GOOD WRITING

IS LIKE

GOOD SEX

* * * *

SORT OF SEXY THOUGHTS ON WRITING

* * * *

C. S. Johnson

C. S. JOHNSON

Copyright © 2019 by C. S. Johnson.

All rights reserved. This book or any portion thereof may not be reproduced or used in any manner whatsoever without the express written permission of the publisher.

1st Edition.
March 31st, 2019.

Ebook ISBN: 978-1-948464-27-7
Paperback ISBN: 978-1-948464-28-4

C. S. JOHNSON

AUTHOR'S ADVISORY NOTE:

Believe it or not, despite the title, this book is relatively clean. I do not talk graphically or personally about sex in this book. You do not need to have had sex to understand this book, and this book is *not* a reason for you to go and have sex, or more sex -- just as reading about the history of drinking should not encourage you to go out and get drunk. However, since it is about sex in general, parents should encourage their younger writers-to-be to read something else. This book is, on average, appropriate for sixteen years of age and up, but I leave it up to the reader and possibly other appropriate parties to decide what is best.

AUTHOR'S ADVISORY NOTE TRANSLATION:

If you read this book and you don't understand it or you are scarred by it, it's not my fault for writing it; it's your fault for reading it.

C. S. JOHNSON

This book is dedicated to my husband. I thought it was romance that would teach me about marriage, but it is marriage that has taught me so much about romance.

This book is also for my most ardent fans. I have to apologize for some of the stuff I say in here, no doubt, but in all seriousness, and in all fun, thank you for your devotion to my work. It is such a comfort to me in dark days, and, during the sunny moments of my life, it makes my world shine even brighter.

C. S. JOHNSON

TABLE OF CONTENTS

PREFACE: *LET'S TALK ABOUT SEX, BABY! (SORT OF)*

CHAPTER 1: *GOOD WRITING IS LIKE GOOD SEX*

CHATPER 2: *A PERSONAL PREP TALK*

CHAPTER 3: *IMPORTANT FUNDAMENTALS FOR DOING IT*

CHAPTER 4: *NOVEL EXPERIENCES*

CHAPTER 5: *SEXY CHARACTERS*

CHAPTER 6: *TENSION AND CONFLICT*

CHATPER 7: *DON'T PICK YOUR NOSE WHILE MAKING OUT*

CHAPTER 8: *GETTING KINKY WTIH IT*

CHAPTER 9: *FINISHING WELL*

CHAPTER 10: *AFTERGLOW*

AUTHOR'S NOTE

ABOUT THE AUTHOR

ABOUT THE EDITOR

SAMPLE READING

PREFACE
* * * *

Let's Talk About Sex, Baby! (Sort of)
You Know You Want To

Have You Ever had A Mental Orgasm?

I always secretly smirk when someone tells me one of my books have given them all the "feelz," because that's when I have to stop myself from saying, "So glad to hear my book gave you a mental orgasm."
I would never actually say that. Never. *Never.*
Aloud or to their face, anyway.
I am a prude, after all, and anyone I went to high school with, perhaps especially my last boyfriend, will tell you so.
But yes, in the merry-go-round inside of my mind, I use the term "mental orgasm," and I think it's funny. I also think it's true, because good writing is like good sex.
If you've ever read a book and it stayed with you as you closed the cover, if you've ever found a story that haunted you for days after you finished it, if you've ever been left simultaneously satisfied and still hungry for more of an imaginary world you left behind—chances are you have experienced a mental orgasm.
Books can certainly blow your mind.
As someone who writes books, and certainly as someone who wants to make an income from writing books, I have had a lot of people ask me about how to write a story and make it into a book, and this book is my edited, more tongue-in-cheek response.

Is This Book for You?

I wrote this book because it's something I think is true and funny, but I didn't write it just to read my own thoughts back to myself. I can write fiction for that, and I would likely be more entertained if I did that; you may also be more entertained if you read my fiction books, which I highly recommend, if I do say so myself.

I wrote this book specifically for people who want to become good fiction writers. While I have to admit you could also read this in hopes of being a better nonfiction writer, I doubt I would consider the following mix of wit and wisdom necessary if I was writing a dissertation or a master's thesis. Maybe if you're going to the Kinsey Institute, but other than that, this book was written with the intent to help storytellers tell better stories in a fun and irreverent, yet deeply respectful sort of way.

Given that it is written by me and I am a prude, as I've already mentioned, this book is not graphic (See Author's Advisory Note). I am a non-gratuitous fiction writer.

However, given that the topic of writing is discussed in comparison to sex, and sex can be a difficult topic for some individuals to discuss (especially on a competent and mature level), this book might be better suited for a writer over the age of sixteen. There are, as I well know from my exemplary search engine skills, a lot of other highly recommended books out there that discuss the topic of how to write better without making silly innuendos every other paragraph or so.

But, if you have taken adequate consideration of yourself, and you feel you are able to handle the topics of writing and sex in a theoretical, educational manner—then welcome to my book.

I hope it gives you the satisfaction you are looking for.

Let Me Entertain You

Before I get into all the fun, and the funny parts of fun, I want to start off by reaffirming my foundation; I have taught English and writing in the classroom for many years on multiple levels, though never from this particular angle. From my teaching experience, I know the importance of doing it right, as it were.

I am C. S. Johnson (CJ to my email buddies) and I am an award-winning, genre-hopping author of several novels. For a little over five years now, I've written fantasy, science fiction, historical fiction, and fairy tales, just to name a few of my favorite genres. I write mostly young adult fiction, but I have also written new adult fiction.

Before I became a writer, I was a teacher. Teaching, like writing, is more of an art than a science. However, unlike writing, teaching was not a particularly joyful pursuit for me. My job eventually became a mountain I'd paid $60,000 or more to climb, only to get halfway up there and realize I never actually wanted to be there in the first place. As soon as I could, I tucked my teaching tools away in an honorable manner than my father never fully approved of, and turned to embrace writing as my true love.

Like Gomer returning to Hosea, I have clung to that love. My very soul demands it after the punishment I have endured, prostituting myself as a teacher as long as I did. Since then, I have learned all I could from my experiences, all in hopes of honoring the thing that saved me from a life of internal dishonor and public damnation.

Everything in this book is what I have learned from the culmination of my education, experiences, and observations, coupled with my own shifting sense of humor and paired with my ambition and passion. My ambition and passion are often synonymous, and I finally have learned to stop apologizing for them.

What You will Find in This Book

This book works through the process of writing preparation, writing itself, and specific areas of content and story development. While there are many people who have asked me about publishing, that topic is very broad; it is like asking me about relationship advice, now that I am married. That's part of the reason I find the similarity between writing and sex both appealing and amusing. From my experience, there are a lot of parallels we can enjoy learning from along the way.

The chapters in this book work through specific elements of writing fundamentals, offering insights into starting out as a writer, adapting your style, building tension, maintaining flow, and providing references for additional help to develop your craft.

I am more confident that you will pay attention to this book than a lot of my high school and college students, because while I am talking about all of these things, I am also talking about sex, and how understanding sex can help you better understand writing. (I may also mention food, naps, science, personal anecdotes, and pop culture to help illustrate my points, but as James Spader's character, Robert California, oh-so-astutely states on *The Office*: "Everything is sex.")

What You will NOT Find in This Book

Everything in this book is from an informed perspective regarding writing. This book has no guarantees to make you a better writer.

Repeat: This book makes no guarantee that you become a better writer just by reading this book.

But while this book and its metaphors make no promises, I can honestly say that, if nothing else, you should get a few laughs out of it.

I've mentioned this a few times, but I will also repeat it here just for clarity: There is nothing explicit in this book.

Repeat: There is nothing explicit in this book.

With regards to the more provocative, sexual side of it, I don't know if it will make you a better lover, but awareness of something is the first step toward improvement or progress, so it can't hurt (or, perhaps it will, depending on what you think of Chapter 8).

I speak on the personal issue of sex as a real-life fairy tale princess. My husband is my knight in shining armor, and I've never doubted his love or his loyalty to me. He's helped me both slay dragons and clean up their poo when I bring them home to try to keep them as pets, and I'm wonderfully ecstatic about getting to spend the rest of my life with him.

I used to think that romance would teach me about marriage, but it's actually marriage that has taught me about romance. From a teaching perspective, it is better to learn what is good from the good, rather than learning what the good is not. This method of instruction is known as "learning by example" and "learning by non-example."

And speaking of the "non" part, I come to my final point in this section: This is a non-judgmental book.

I am *not* here to pass judgment on your characters—or you.

You can be as personally liberal or as conservative as you like when it comes to sex. This is not about politics, although that angle might come out in your work. Sex itself is something that conservatives must acknowledge and something that liberals must acknowledge has limits. I truly believe that everyone—*everyone*—is a conservative about something, just as everyone is liberal about something—whether it's your time, your money, your morals, your diet, or your love.

I am writing from an informed standpoint regarding writing. There will always be certain requirements for good writing, and that will never change, no matter how much sex is liberalized. There are always going to be people who read your work who will rightfully expect certain things out of it in order to find it "good."

Nothing in this book should be taken as a personal attack on you. It is also not an attack on any group of people, living or dead, alien or even imaginary, and anything read into the text by a hostile or ignorant audience should be *immediately* disregarded.

So, with that in mind, let's go and take a cold shower, and then dive into this thing, shall we?

CHAPTER 1
* * * *

Good Writing is Like Good Sex
Intellectual Foreplay

What makes a book sexy?

I'm not talking about erotica. What is the difference between a book you eagerly devour and a book you slum your way through? Sometimes you can see this in movies, too—what is the difference between a movie you can get excited about watching over and over again and a movie that's more "meh," or that you put in those "ironically bad" or "watch with friends while high/drinking/avoiding work" categories to make it bearable?

While there are often extenuating circumstances or exceptional conditions regarding each book or individual film, the most objective difference between a really great story and downright terrible story is simple.

It comes down to the *writing*.

It's either good writing, and we can forgive the technical flaws a little more easily, or it's bad writing, and it's worth every moment of our second-by-second break down of our all-encompassing contempt.

Bad writing is just bad.

Good writing, on the other hand, taunts you, intrigues you, and calls to you; it pulls at your heart and slips inside your soul. It seduces your mind, letting its words grow into your vernacular, giving rise to new, previously unknown daydreams and desires.

Good writing is sexy.

And because of this, there are several parallels between writing and sex that can enhance the enjoyment of the other, but that is more dependent on you than me. This is good news for us who enjoy a good story and enjoy—or hope to enjoy one day after you get married—good sex.

Sex and writing are both intimate acts of creation, acts which begin inside of us and extend outward to others. While one might begin on the physical level, and the other might begin in the mind, sex and writing both end up reflecting the essence of who we are and hint at the fullness and totality of our lives. These are purposeful acts, acts that have a distinct goal in mind—producing a form of pleasure—and just like good sex, the path to producing good writing actually starts long before you start.

In my historical fiction novel, *Kingdom of Ash and Soot*, one of my characters -- Lady Penelope, a spymaster for Queen Victoria -- has a scene where she is telling Eleanora, my main character, why it is important for her to learn about sex and how to use it to her advantage as a spy. I enjoy this scene because Lady Penelope is very blunt and outspoken, despite the Victorian era's modesty and Eleanora's own obvious discomfort. And while the whole scene is meant to juxtapose their characters while also commencing Eleanora's hero-transformation, what Lady Penelope says is very true:

"Any simpleton can look at a painting or sculpture and know that it is art. But only a true and trained master knows how to create such a splendid pleasure."

Michelangelo didn't come into the world ready to paint the Sistine Chapel, Tolstoy didn't write *War and Peace* just after puberty, and Beethoven didn't just bang his head against the keyboard to write his *Moonlight Sonata*. Learning begins before doing, even if testing sometimes requires doing before learning.

The Difference between Mastery and Success

If you are reading this, it's likely at least one of your main goals is to learn how to write better so you can write books and make a profit selling them. However, having found this trap several times on my own, I want to highlight the difference between mastery and success before I get too far.

What is Mastery?

Mastery is dependent on talent and skill—the act of putting what you have observed and learned down into concrete form.
Mastery is *not* dependent on financial success.
Vincent van Gogh never sold a painting in his lifetime, except one to his brother. No one would have called him a success then. Today, millions of people adore his work. F. Scott Fitzgerald was an alcoholic writer who often struggled with his finances; he died of a heart attack in his forties, thinking he had wasted his life. Today his books are taught in many high school curricula and he is revered as a prominent writer who captured the spirit of the Roaring Twenties.
Mastery is not about money; mastery is about talent and skill.
Once you have your full manuscript, your full act of creation, the talent can be seen in your execution of its creation. The words and phrases you've used,

the structure of your sentences, and your plotline will all be judged on their level of competence, creativity, and conventions.

Again, mastery is *not* about the money. It is possible you will fulfill your full potential as a writer and not make any money from it. While that is unlikely in today's word of technology and self-publishing, it is a possibility you should consider if you are hoping to sell your work.

Writing does not have to be about money, either. If you want to write, and if you want to work hard to master your skill and harness your talent, you are in good company. There are lots of good reasons to write and create—writing to teach, writing to learn, writing to express something nothing else can, writing to understand something you can't process in another way. There are as many reasons writers have for writing as there are writers themselves. Art is a compulsion, like the beating of a heart, or a demon leeching off a soul.

It is a very special thing to share your imagination with others in a way that alters their own.

Mastery is mastering your own ability to create; success is different from mastery.

What is Success?

In the case of success, success can include mastery, but mastery doesn't always include success. This is part of the reason success is both harder and easier to acquire than mastery.

Mastery is much more like a standardized exam, where you can pass or fail, or even exceed the expectations placed on you.

Success, while it can be taken on the universal side (more on that later), it is often something that is more personally applied. Which means, of course, its definition and requirements can change and you don't always notice.

Personal Success

An author friend once asked me what I thought success for me looked like. I did not have an answer at the time. Now, while I can say success is just being able to write, knowing someone, somewhere, has enjoyed my work, I also know that my definition of success can change, and it doesn't always tell me when it wants to change.

"Success" then, becomes a word like "perfect," where we assume it is a fixed, stagnant destination, but instead, it is an ever-growing landscape that can change with every step we take toward it.

To help work through it some more, I would suggest thinking of success in terms of different levels—almost like mastery, but where *you* get to decide what is most important.

Your "Success Level 1" might be just getting the writing done. Lots of people want to write a book, but not everyone does. Writing in itself is a level of success. "Success Level 2" might be publishing your book or getting an agent. Perhaps the more ambitious of us might see our book made into a movie or a TV series as a goal. Maybe it has to do with awards or a certain level of income per month.

Sometimes our success might cross over with mastery, as I mentioned earlier, in that we want our books to be seen as literary works of acclaim for decades to come.

The "Success Trap" can happen to everyone. I recommend you write your goals for success down, so you do not lose sight of what is really important to you. This also helps if you want to add to it later or check something off your list; you will be able to see how far you've come and what else you need to do.

Success and Money

Success is not necessarily about skill level. After all, you can write the greatest book ever written and no one will read it, and it is possible you can write something poorly and sell a lot of copies, regardless. Everyone can name at least *one* book that succeeded commercially that is not actually well written.

Success is not necessarily about finances, either—however, on the more public side of this argument, as opposed to the personal side, there is a more cynical-sounding discussion that revolves around money. That is because sometimes writing often does actually come down to making money. It was Samuel Johnson, the father of the English Dictionary, who said, "Only a fool writes for anything but money."

(To which I laugh in the mirror and reply to his imaginary reflection, "Ah, but the heart has its reasons, whereas reason has lost its mind, Mr. Johnson.")

But Samuel Johnson does have a point. There are benefits to aiming for financial success when you write.

Money provides a motivating external incentive. Even if you were born rich, marry rich, or strike it rich, you will do better as a writer if you get money from your work. There is an added level of confidence that financial reward gives you. Objective, external incentives such as this help inspire the internal motivation we need: courage to keep going, the determination to try harder, and continual resolve to advance our mastery.

Why Would You Buy Your Book?

If you're a writer, or you're looking to be one (God help you), chances are you're not going to give your work away for free. Potential buyers will want to know why they should pay you.

"What's so special about your story?" is the semi-polite shorthand for "Why should I pay you money?"

If you want to build a following, gain a readership, get an income, and earn the recognition and respect of your peers and public audience, you will want to write a story that people will buy, and the more people who buy it and like it, the better.

I know—not from my own experience, so far as you know—that you can only blackmail and guilt people so much into reading your stuff before you run out of people willing to speak with you.

Some Hard Truths

So, what's so special about your book?
What's so special about your story?
If the hero has a thousand faces, why is yours, in particular, the one I should pay attention to?
These are frightening questions. Especially when coupled with the following insights:

1. Nearly anyone can write a book in today's world. I've heard before that roughly 85% of people say they want to write a book. Out of over seven billion people, that means more than six billion people say they want to write a book. How are you different from those six billion plus people? Why should your work stand out among them?

2. Books can be about anything. *Anything.* There are some 87 million people with published books on Amazon (including me) and that means that if you're going to buy a book, you have a lot of choices (even though you should buy mine anyway). Why would someone buy your book?

These are some of the most terrifying questions I have faced as a writer—the ones that always seem to come right before either the elation of acceptance or the despair of rejection.

Some part of me still reflexively chokes up and gets paralyzed by those questions every time I get to pitch my work to potential buyers. It doesn't even matter who it is. Some of my most awkward moments have come from trying to explain my work to family members or friends, but I know what it is like to pitch to the big leagues, too.

Pitching to publishers or Hollywood might be easier, since it's less personal, but it is still pretty hard. They will ask you what makes your story different and what is so special about it that millions of people will choose to give precious moments of their time to it?

What will make investors write their checks and what will encourage the best people in the business to work on developing your story for a movie, television, animation, or comic? If you're going into the really lucrative elements of it, they will ask you what is so special about your work that those people will go out and buy t-shirts, clothes, toys, DVDs, etc. to celebrate their love of your work?

There *is* some good news about this, although it might not seem like it at first.

We Do the Same Thing with Sex

We do the same thing with sex, believe it or not. The form of compensation changes, but the questions are pretty similar, and that's because the same beginning principles apply in regard to sex as they do with writing:

1. Nearly everyone can have sex, and a lot more people can view sexual acts than ever, thanks to magazines, television, and the internet. Today even some objects in your house can have sex. What's so special about you?

2. If you thought 87 million other authors were a lot, right now there around roughly around other 5 billion consenting adults in the world who can have sex.

If you grew up worried that no one would ever know the real you, let alone love the real you enough to want to marry the real you, or maybe even if you feel like that now, these are also scary statistics. Of course, statistics tend to be terrifying in general.

But here is where good sex and good writing have a lot in common, which can offer a great deal of relief when it comes to being a writer.

Here's the good news:

1. **Good sex comes with limits. After all, there is such a thing as bad sex.**

    Just like you would not want to fall in love with, and marry, and have sex with everyone in the world, you most likely don't want to write something everyone in the world will read. God is obviously the big exception to this, of course, but for us mere mortals, not everyone is suited for romance, not everyone wants a mystery, or violence, or war, or Amish robots battling against zombie superheroes just outside the gates of hell, etc.

    Not everyone wants the things that you write.

    And please note, your attempts to please everyone *will* be counterproductive. I see this all the time: when writers attempt to please their fandoms at length, the writers soon lose their way and no one, except possibly the loudest, most obnoxious critic in the room will be happy, and if you are the loudest, most obnoxious critic in the room, you are probably not a happy person.

If you think I am wrong about this, all you have to do is tell five people you love the most you are taking them all out to dinner together, and they get to decide where—so long as they are in complete agreement. Anyone who has a family should be laughing at this moment, because getting five people to agree on where to eat just about never happens, despite any Olive Garden marketing campaigns you've seen.

You will have a much easier time, and a much more pleasant experience, if you just tell them that you are going to take them with you to a restaurant of your choice. If they do not want to go, they can stay at home, and you will not have to worry about them making the experience less pleasant for the people who do want to go.

The same thing needs to happen with our writing. We will discuss this more in Chapter 4.

2. **Good sex is special.**

When you look at you and your spouse, or Bella and Edward, or Romeo and Juliet, or Jamie and Claire from *Outlander* ... why is sex so special when it comes to them? Why do we root for them to be bonded together in this way?

In novels, we have shorthand signals for this. Sex often represents, in these love stories, true love between two people. There is often a selection of physical, scientific, biological, sociological, psychological, and religious reasons that support our story's favorite characters in getting together.

Most characters, for example, are physically attractive. Emotionally, they seem like good people, or people we can cheer for. Mentally, a lot of their appeal in the idea of love conquering all things and breaking through any barriers. And spiritually, we all long for those same things: we long to be wanted, we long to be needed, we long to feel complete.

And that is why it is special when they come together. They are in love—in deep, everlasting, all-consuming love -- the kind that makes you grab the one you're destined to spend the rest of your life with with all your strength, forcing the last constraints of your flesh against theirs in hopes that your bare souls can touch.

Sex is not ever "just sex." The process of communication has eight stages—yes, really, talking to someone is actually that complicated—so it should not be surprising to find out that sex is more complicated than just "doing it." It is a physical, emotional, mental, and spiritual act.

Sex is good when it has consideration for all of these elements. A good story should strive to do the same.

You don't just fall in love with anyone. You fall in love with someone special.

3. **Good sex gets better with *intentional* practice.**

The saying goes that "practice makes perfect," but I tend to agree more with the version that says, "practice makes permanent." If you practice making cakes with dog poo in them, you're always going to have a bad product, even if you add more sugar and throw on extra rainbow sprinkles.

So, practice doesn't make perfect, unless that practice is intentionally focused on improvement.

Both sex and writing get better when you are intentional about optimizing your performance, and that includes practicing. No matter how talented someone is as a writer—because there is a natural talent that some people are really just born with—dedication to their craft will always allow them to get better.

Caveats and Provisos

Now, here is where the metaphor has to deviate a little, and some distinctions must be made, especially by those of us who feel like nuance is a lost art and the moral backbone must have its say.

You want to write a book that a reader will fall in love with, a book they will want to spend time with, a book they will purchase—a book that they will call their own.

This is not the same as selecting a spouse, or chasing down a lover, or paying for sex, just as experiencing an emotional catharsis from a book is not the same as a sexual climax. You are not inappropriately whoring your talent out for attention and fame by writing. You wouldn't say working as an ice cream maker is inappropriate when he or she sells his or her ice cream, for example, even though sharing our own creations with others is an intensely personal and intentionally pleasurable experience.

Now that We've Cleaned Up, Back to Business …

Nearly everyone can write. Nearly everyone can have sex. But it takes true love, devotion, hard work, and tapping into your uniqueness that take it beyond the act itself—to the culmination of true love, hard work, dedicated attention, and deep, abiding faith.

Good writing is like good sex. It's part mental, part emotional, part physical, and part spiritual. Your story is a piece of your heart, mind, and soul that gets wrapped up in language and sent out into the world for the world's perusal, enjoyment, and perhaps even betterment.

Good sex allows us to become better people and artists; in fact, the end biological goal of sex is reproduction, where our bodies can literally create something that has the power to change the world. In many ways, good sex has the beloved and the lover as both teacher and student, reinforcing our love for another and affirming the good things another loves about us.

When it comes to writing your book, your book *will* be special. You are providing an experience or perspective—one you've created—that is unique, just because you are you.

And "You" is a really good place to start.

CHAPTER 2

* * * *

A Personal Prep Talk
Taking a Personal Inventory

"So, what's so special about your book?"

It's still a terrifying question, but the more you see it, the better you can prepare to answer it.

It might be hard for you to realize that your book is special at all, especially if you are a new writer, or you're one of those people who struggle with self-confidence (I can assure you from personal experience you are in good company). I know exactly how that feels.

But your book *will* be special, because it's *yours*.

It is your words written down on paper, your story written for the world to see, and the book you were born to write.

It's *yours*.

This is something that people tend to say about kids, and I like using this analogy here because kids can be the result of good sex, just as my "book babies" are the result of my writing. No one will love my real children the way I do. My kids are unlike everyone else's children because they are mine. And no one will ever love my husband the way I do, because he is the one I chose and the one who chose me back. Your own love story will be special because it's yours.

Your book will be special too.

But, let's face it, "special" has its limits, especially when it comes to the competitive writing market.

Your unique outlook should be what tips the balance in your favor, and you do yourself a lot of favors if your tipping point doesn't have a lot of unattractive baggage dragging it down. This means you need to take care to make your book be its best.

Here are some key things to keep in mind while you work on developing your book.

<u>Your Special You</u>

1. Don't Be Afraid to Be Yourself: respect the power you have as a writer

In the course of my years as a writer, I have had a lot of people tell me they are thinking about writing a book, but they don't know if they will be good enough or if the story is actually something good for them to write.

This concern comes up a lot when writing about "harder topics," come up. One example from my own life I've struggled to talk about is my experience with depression. This is harder to explain in some circles more than others, especially when there are days when you wonder if there will be a happily ever after. Some people are uncomfortable with that, and they should be, in all fairness; dealing with depression and all its side effects, some of which are strange and others which are extremely varied, is not something you are born knowing how to handle. It gets worse when you are surprised (a lot of people, I think, who know me know I like to laugh and have fun.) That is part of the reason I've used elements of my own experience in my work (of all the book of my Starlight Chronicles series, I still cry the most at the end of *Outpouring*). I want people to be able to understand me and my experience with depression better.

Frankly, I myself wanted to understand my depression better, and writing about it really helped—and that is why I encourage people not to shy away from writing about harder topics, even if there is a place for restraint. I know it can hurt, like cleaning a wound; but I also know it can help.

Everyone is unique in the life that they have lived. While there are some experiences I may never know the directly, writers are the perfect people to use language to convey that experience to me in a way I can clearly imagine. From that, empathy and understanding are born, and that helps connect us to each other. While you may have never experienced depression, reading about it through a character would ideally provide new insight. You've likely heard of the term "second-hand smoke." This is a form of "second-hand experience."

When you go to write your story, embrace what is unique about your life. Maybe it's a physical feature you have, maybe it's something you've experienced or something you've set out to accomplish. Maybe it's not something you've done or something you've had, but something you want. Maybe it's something more than that— maybe it's something you love, something you hate, or something you just want to learn more about, and putting it into a story seems like an interesting way to do so.

In terms of sex, I would compare this aspect of writing to your personality.

You are who you are due to nature and nurture—both have their limitations and their exceptions, but you have the choice to change a lot about who you are regardless of either nature or nurture. How would other people describe you? What is something you overcame? What have you learned through your life?

You bring your personality to your sexual experience with your partner, and you should use your life experience and what you have learned from it to make your story.

A Quick Caveat

Many people use stories as a place to preach or to gain the moral high ground on someone else, and unless you are a pastor or religious figure, this can be *inconvenient* to your audience (there are other not-as-nice adjectives I could use, but I'll leave it there).

Too many books and movies, and even commercials in recent years, have come down to lessons on why you should or shouldn't do/think/believe something.

The other side of this, where a writer indulges in the full extent of his or her fantasies, can be just as grotesque. Excessive description— gore, sex, violence, etc.—can easily take away from the overall story.

As a fiction writer, you are there to tell a story. You are there to provide an emotional experience and transcribe the experiences of a character, or even multiple characters. If you do this well enough, you won't have to be explicit about the moral of the story; it will come through on its own. Yes, there will probably be people who will miss it. But it is still better to write the story well enough, and make it palpable enough, that more people will want to read it (I speak from personal experience on this one.)

From an English teacher's point of view, not all readers will walk away with the lesson you intend them to learn if you want them to leave with something more than just a story. If you want to use a book as a soapbox, that's your prerogative. If you use it to indulge in your fantasies, that's your choice. But it will narrow the people who will be interested in hearing what you say. I am not saying you can't do it; I am saying if you do decide to do it, do it well enough that people -- even if they disagree with your work -- will be adequately entertained.

This is a caveat you should consider very deeply and thoroughly before publishing your work and sending it out into the world, and this bleeds over into my next point:

2. Be Flexible, But Sure: modification is not the same thing as selling out (but it can be)

One of my own weaknesses as a writer is remaining utterly stubborn about my work. When someone offers a suggestion, it can feel like unwarranted criticism or a personal attack. Writing is very personal, after all, and growing a thick skin takes an insane amount of practice for the soft-hearted. But as any seasoned writer will tell you, even the most exceptional ones do not produce perfect work, nor do they publish all their work. Feedback, good and bad, can help produce better work. There is bad work, good work, and better work.

If you are getting feedback on your writing that is not positive, then you may need to change something to make the emotional experience your readers get more satisfying, or make the storyline more logical and believable.

When I first started writing, my books could do no wrong. They were perfect. But if I read through them now, I can easily spot a few things that could be tweaked or changed for the better. Fortunately, I had a lot of good feedback from different people that helped me in the beginning.

This happens with sex, too. You shouldn't feel personally attacked if your partner asks for something new or asks you to try something a different way, or maybe in a different place.

For your writing, you should not feel like suggestions for changes are personal attacks, or that making things to market standards is "selling out." You bring your life experiences to the table when you set out to write a story, but tweaking it to help people better understand it, enjoy it, or buy it is not the same thing as selling out—necessarily.

There is a limit to this one, too.

One of the more controversial things in traditional publishing is how, in most contracts, your publisher can make you add specific changes to your work. I always encourage people to think through such suggestions, but never compromise your convictions. Readers, especially readers who know your work, will likely know the difference between your own work and work that you have changed to appease your publisher.

On the indie publishing side, one of the biggest dangers I've found of the "write to market" crowd is that it can quickly devolve into the "write to please" market. While expectations are good for structure, too much structure can be dehumanizing. (If you've ever heard of a story being too "formulaic," you know what I mean.) If you are writing the same story with different character names and maybe a different location or two, that's not great writing. That's marketable writing that's lazy—and that's where "selling out" begins, when you allow too much of the market or too many of your fans to determine changes to your work (especially if you feel pressured to do so for financial reward). There is a difference between the audience making requirements for reading your work and your audience enjoying the work you've chosen to alter for their enjoyment.

This is true on a physical level when it comes to sex. A lot of sex is portrayed in the media as sex between toned, muscled-up parties. But real sex means that some women will have stretch marks, some men will be overweight, and both parties run the risk of bad breath. Some people have rules or a routine that they follow when they engage in sexual relationships—but we all know that we're looking for the relationship that will make those people break their rules.

I'll talk more about making your work more attractive in the next chapter. For now, we are discussing your personal approach to writing.

3. Be Strong, But Smart: establish good practices—and practice good boundaries

One of the things that is pretty easy to say is that you should work on your writing.

One of the harder parts of being a writer is that it is not a traditional job. You probably don't have an office you go to everyday to write. You are your own boss. You have to provide a lot of your own measurements for quality. Your deadlines for projects can be much more flexible.

Because you don't have a traditional job, more people see your time as expendable or adaptable to their needs, so you have to make a plan to work, and then you have to work to make sure you keep to your plan. This means establishing a good structure and encouraging good boundaries between writing and the rest of your life.

Most authors I know rely on time, effort, or finished product results when they work on their writing.

> **Time:** Some writers will carve out a number of hours of the day (or week) to write. Using time can help establish a routine, and routines allow us to quickly adapt to our needs. Determine a time of day that you can write. Hopefully you will have a place to write, but even sitting with a notebook or at the computer can help get you ready to write.
>
> Everything you decide to do with your time has a price. In choosing to write, you are also choosing not to do something else. If you want to be a good writer, you have to put in the time. Use that time wisely.
>
> **Effort:** Effort is trickier to measure, because it is subjective from person to person.

Different projects definitely require different amount of effort. And some writing will be easier just because you love it more or because you are more confident with your direction. Love makes work lighter, as does confidence in your output.

Finished Results: Pick something you want to finish, and then don't stop until you finish it.

That one is pretty self-explanatory.

Boundaries are not just there to help establish good practices. They are there to encourage healthy execution. Failing to keep good practices often comes from the deficiencies and overabundances we have on our boundaries. This means that you should work hard to satisfy your standards—and even exceed them, if you can—but the key word in that is "work."

If you're going by time, don't let anyone interrupt your time. Don't be too eager to leave your post at the smallest distraction, and if something comes up that demands your immediate response—such as a family matter—schedule a make-up shift. Learn to say no to the things that are not as important to you as your writing.

If you're going by effort, give yourself writing requirements specific to each project. Write something, edit something, outline something. Do what you set out to do, and then tackle it with the most energy and excitement you can. Here, some sexual advice can also apply: fake it till you make it. Sometimes it can take a while to warm up, and there's no shame in that; it ultimately means there's a good chance there's more fun and more of a payout in the end.

If you use finished results as your goal, prepare appropriate and realistic deadlines. Make sure any contractors you might have are on time. Adapt as needed.

Simply put: Don't be a lazy soft-hearted excuse-maker, but don't be a heartless overachieving self-slave-driving perfectionist, either.

Everyone has a story, but your story won't get written unless you write it.

Once you've written it, you can worry about whether or not it has "sex appeal," which is the topic for the next chapter.

But now that you've thought of your story, made the choice to write it, made a plan to get started, it is time to hold your head high, take a deep breath, and plunge forward into the next step.

This is where you have to work hard *and* work smart. When people ask you the question about whether you're working harder or smarter, you need to smirk up at that schmuck and say, "Both."

With that in mind, it's time to review the basic mechanics of good writing.

CHAPTER 3
* * * *

Important Fundamentals for Doing It
Sexy Writing Basics

Good writing and good sex both start with having a solid understanding of the basics. Do you have the basics down? Socrates once said that the unexamined life is not worth living, and I'm more than happy to contend that the unexamined manuscript is not worth reading. Good, sexy writing looks effortless, and that is part of the reason everyone thinks he can do it with ease. But good writing is hardly effortless if you have to squint your eyes to see past the obvious mistakes.

The same thing is true of sex—making it look easy doesn't mean that it is.

Up till this point in the book, I've talked about why I am more or less qualified to write this book (always a plus), I've gone over some of the numbers (which I am sure will change, even as I write this), and I've admitted there are risks and doubts and fears in front of you --I've even warned you that there will be sacrifice, hard work, and tough choices in the near future for the fiction writer-to-be when it comes to writing your story and getting it fully written.

Now it is time to trick you into more work with a sexy grammar review. After analyzing yourself for your best features and taking apart your personal baggage inventory, it's time to get to work.

<u>Standards are Sexy (Yes, Really)</u>

There are general things that everyone looks for in a good book, just like there are general things that people look for in a good mate. While you definitely have your own uniqueness, there are steps you can take on the outside to ensure that more people take notice and appreciate the intricacies of your work as a whole—and as much as we like to think we're not shallow, some of that shallowness has a deep point.

As we see in fairy tales, the outward appearance is representative of the inner character. Of course, humanity is a little more complex than fairy tales, and people have enough trouble with fairy tales. Beauty can be deceptive in this way, but if our work is beautiful on the outside, we are more likely to excuse some of the inner disarray. How many "good girls" are really attracted to ugly-looking "bad boys," after all? Chances are they see the outward appearance of a fallen angel and when faced with the internal mess of a soul said fallen angel may have, the girls want to clean it up.

Outward appearances signal to us what is on the inside. We all want to fall in love with someone we can trust, for example, and there are things you can do to show you are trustworthy: being on time, keeping your promises, consistency in temperament. We also want to fall in love with people who are responsible, and there are ways to physically demonstrate this characteristic—for example, taking care of a sick person, maintaining a job, or keeping up good grades. Think of the ugly girl who needs to take off her glasses and get a makeover so the handsome guy will notice her, or consider the knight in shining armor who has to be able to fight off his princess's dragons. Your book's inner beauty should be reflected in the outward appearance of your story—

these outward appearance tweaks can be seen in grammar, mechanics, and formatting.

Gaining and Losing Sex Appeal

Grammar is the good hygiene of sexy writing. You could be the sexiest woman alive but if you don't brush your teeth, comb your hair, wear acceptable or even nice-looking clothes, your one true love could easily pass you by. You could also be the most handsome and most virtuous of men, but if you don't cut your toenails once in a while, you could miss out on so much.

The same thing applies to writing. You could have the best story in the world, but if it isn't written with good grammar, if it doesn't look attractive, someone is going to complain while someone else might dismiss it up front.

And even if they don't, those small grammatical errors could be the difference between a four-star rating and a five-star rating when another someone is finished examining your work.

Grammar is a larger topic, here are a few of the bigger issues that tend to ruin a reader's afternoon delight:

1. **Sentences**

While it may seem pretty basic, make sure you write your story using full sentences. There are occasions when you can use an incomplete sentence. When you need the emphasis. When you need to be dramatic. When you run out of ideas. When you're trying to capture a particular tone.

But generally speaking, save it for when you really need it. Aim for writing full, complete sentences, with a subject (or subjects) and a predicate (or predicates).

Be sure to add a period at the end of the sentence to show that you're finished writing

Otherwise it'll look weird. Trust me on this one. (Hint, hint, wink, wink, smirk.) This topic is also discussed further along in mechanics, where punctuation is prime.

2. Parts of Speech

A good sentence is made when the writer properly uses the parts of speech. This one might be a little harder, since there are eight parts of speech.

1) **Nouns** are people, places, and things. Personal nouns refer to specific names for people.

    Nana baked *cookies* at my *house.*

2) **Verbs** show action or being.

    I *yell* when a slow car *is driving* in the passing lane.

3) **Pronouns** replace the personal nouns.

   John's backpack was ugly.
   His lunchbox was acceptable.

4) **Adjectives** describe nouns or pronouns.

   My shirt is *blue*.

5) **Adverbs** describe verbs, adjectives, or other adverbs.

   My examples are written out *carefully*.

6) **Prepositions** link ideas between nouns and pronouns.

   The ants crawled *into* the anthill.
   I went walking *in* the woods.

7) **Conjunctions** link nouns, sentences, and incomplete sentences together.

   People *and* animals may not have a lot in common, *but* I couldn't think of a better sentence than this one to illustrate this concept.

8) **Interjections** interrupt your sentence -- or can be their own sentence, and it convey emotional emphasis.

Hey! Hey, don't you know what an interjection is?

These can be tricky because it's more of how a word is used rather than the word itself. Several words can be used as either nouns or verbs depending on their use and placement in the sentence.

Example: My jump was the highest; I jump the highest.

But the basic point of this review was to get you to think about how to use words correctly—because using your words correctly will allow you to use them effectively—when you are writing your story.

3. **Mechanics**

Mechanics refers to the extra conditions and marks you will use to put all your words together. I've already mentioned the period, but there are commas, and semicolons, and quotation marks, and other ending markings; and then there are capital letters for names and the beginning of your sentences, apostrophes for showing ownership or contractions, and parentheses, for enclosing side remarks (because where would I be without the side remarks?).

All of this might seem simple—but then, a kiss is just a kiss until it's more than just a kiss. Things that seem small become more important as they become part of something larger. One kiss might not seem like much in the process of seduction; but when the final act has been finished, each kiss can be seen as a stepping stone into the larger emotional experience.

The same thing happens with writing. When people read, a well-placed semicolon is the titillating promise that more is to come; a period is an aching sadness until the next sentence sparks joy. Making sure your sentences are clear, properly put together, and complete is just the same as combing your hair, brushing your teeth, and shaving your legs before you and your partner get it on. It's the little things that can really add so much more thrill to the overall experience.

For assistance with this, hiring a qualified line editor can really do wonders for your work. Editors are the great photoshoppers of writing. They trim the fat, add the poof, check the lighting, and add a dash of professionalism to your work.

You should work hard to make your writing look its best. However, work by itself is no guarantee it will be good or better than good. If you tweak something about your body, you don't know if it will have a positive impact or not. Suppose a man gets hair plugs, or say a woman gets a nose job. Maybe they will look better, but it is also possible they will look worse.

While this chapter covered the play-by-play of the word-by-word basics of good *writing*, it's time to dive into the content of your *story* itself.

CHAPTER 4
*   *   *   *

Novel Experiences
Romancing the Reader

Right here seems to be the best place to remind you of something important: real life is different from imaginary life.

Real life and imagination are brought together in you, in your own personal life experience. This is why C. S. Lewis called man "the great amphibian." We, as humans, live cognizant lives because our brains are able to translate our sensory experiences and our bodily responses into the fabric of what we call a life. There is a meeting of the mental, physical, emotional, and spiritual sides of who we are in our bodies, most particularly our minds.

These are all real parts of ourselves, and I can prove it to you.

Mentally, you should be able to process the words I am writing on this page into a coherent thought. You should be able to read these words; if you are hearing them, you should be able to determine what I am saying by the sequence of letters and words I am typing on this page. You should also be able to determine if I am insulting you are not, should I actually do so.

Physically, you should be able to experience this book in some manner. You can see it, you can touch it, I don't recommend tasting it but you can certainly try, you can listen to someone read these words aloud, and you can sniff it—watch out for the glue on the paperback binding, please. I'm here to make you excited for writing, not something else.

Emotionally and spiritually are the two that seem to be the most confusing for people to separate, although it is also tied into the mental state, too.

The emotional reaction to something is just that: how something makes you feel. The spiritual reaction is more your reaction to your emotions. For example, if I read your work and tell you it's crap but you can fix it, you might be angry or depressed; that is the emotional reaction. The spiritual reaction is clear when you decide what to do. You can, at that point, buckle down and do better, or you can decide to give up and go back to law school, like your mother would prefer. Some people mistake this for mentality, but it is more than that, because this inner resolve translates into what you do; it is a deep-seated response, calling out for supernatural or metaphysical aid as you work to do what is right, not what is easy or convenient.

So those are all real parts of yourself, and all the sides of yourself crash together in your body, and your body is where life meets you, and you experience life as well as live it. Paradoxes are not the same as contradictions—which is a line from *Prince of Secrets and Shadows,* another one of my novels. Not that you'll necessarily want to buy that one after reading this one, of course. (But you should anyway).

Try as you might, you cannot just live life inside your mind, and you would be very hard-pressed to live your life without using your brain. (I'm sure some people manage to do this, but I digress.) While you are reading this, you are actually proving this statement true. You are reading this using your mind, sitting in a physical world that surrounds you which includes other people who are also able to experience the physical world around you. If you show this page to someone else, and they can read, they would be able to read this the same as you, but they might read this and have a different reaction to it than you. (Hopefully neither of you are eager to come hunt me down and kill me.)

Christian apologist Ravi Zacharias once said that people cannot live completely objective lives, and neither can they live completely subjective lives, and I am certain that if you attempt to do just that, you will likely fail.

Your job as a writer is to create an emotional experience for the reader—an emotional experience that you will decide on and one you can refine through creative intent—but one that will have to make sense, and further allow the reader to make sense of his or her own life.

When I was first learning about poetry, there were two definitions from writers that were used to describe it:

Poetry is *"what is often thought, but ne'er so well expressed,"* according to Alexander Pope.

For William Wordsworth, poetry was *"emotion reflected in tranquility."*

Since poetry is among the most refined examples of writing, this same principle can apply here. There are two fundamental positions that writing begins from—a logical, intellectual, and wise foundation of universal truth, and an emotional, specific, and personal instance.

Real life and imagination work together to perpetuate and enhance our experience with life as much as they are needed to create it; I like to think of it as a strand of theoretical DNA, where one is complemented by the other, and they are held together with little inklings of both the natural and the supernatural.

But you must remember that real life and imagination are fundamentally different from each other. This is true no matter what kind of fiction story you decide to write, and applies across all genres.

Writing: A True but Fake Experience

Because writing is an act of creation that requires the mental, physical, spiritual, and emotional facilities, it's good to point out that there are certain things about stories that do not happen in real life.

1. As a sense-making device, stories should make sense. (Real life does not always make sense.)
2. As an emotional experience, stories should cause an emotional reaction in the reader. (The one you intend might be different from the resulting emotional output. Real life does not always follow our plans, even when we write the script.)

Keeping the earlier "theoretical DNA" picture in mind, your job is to take elements of real life and imagination and build those small links of a twisted bridge together into a new creation. In this way, it is like creating a form of story-formed Splenda: not the same thing as real sugar -- possibly healthier, but also fake with different side effects.

When you begin to write your story, you are working on building up a full, readable experience. To live a life dedicated to love means more than just sex, even if sex is very fun and happy and matters a great deal to the overall quality of your life. This same principle applies to your writing.

If you're going to have good sex, you have to realize that good sex is more than just good sex.

If you want to have good sex in real life, you have to meet someone that you're interested in, you should build up a relationship between yourself and that person so they will be interested in you as well and you will be able to earn their trust, and then as you fall in love, you should raise the stakes, so to speak, and take the relationship up to advanced levels that include sex and likely other things as well (marriage, children, joint social media accounts—Ha! Just kidding on that last one).

When it comes to good writing, the same principles apply.

What Kind of Reader are You Romancing?

While this book uses good sex as a vehicle for understanding good writing, not all books are romance novels, obviously. But it is a good metaphor to use when you think of the relationship between you, the author, and your intended audience.

Because real life and imagination are different, there are a different set of expectations for them. This is easily demonstrated when you imagine sex and when you actively engage in sex. When you are a writer, you are creating a real but fake experience, and you are bringing it to life with words. The reader, in picking up the book, already agrees to those terms; it would be very strange for a book to open up and transport us to a new world (though it would be awesome!) where we live out the story ourselves. Romancing the reader then becomes a job of meeting or exceeding their expectations. If you wanted to go on a date with someone, you would plan it out so they would not only enjoy themselves, but they would be pleasantly surprised. A nice dinner, a good movie, and then a surprise trip for ice cream or coffee before a romantic, thoughtful goodnight kiss?

Yes, please. This date of yours will want a second one.

When it comes to writing, we all hope to do this with the readers who read our stories. When you write and publish books, they should want *more* from you, and the same, though still a little different.

Audience Awareness

I should clarify two things before going deeper with this topic.

First, you are writing each story for a particular audience. That audience can change over time, or you can swap it out for another one as you work on different stories. Plenty of famous writers have shifted their audiences to new ones, whether it is a change in genre (maybe you want mystery instead of romance to take precedence), a shift in age (are you writing more middle grade or young adult?), or perhaps even in style (are you using higher vocabulary or expletives?).

It is entirely possible that your audience will remain the same over time, too. Many books with a formulaic feel to them, especially by the same author, have a consistent audience core.

When you go out to mingle, or when you go somewhere to possibly find a date, or someone you're interested in, you will not likely go to the same place every night wearing the same thing or looking the same way. You'll at least change your clothes and periodically you'll get a haircut. Maybe you'll even get a new car to drive you there. When you start writing a book, it is the same thing. You're working on making yourself look a certain way in hopes of attracting certain people. You may practice some pick-up lines in the mirror ("Hey there, have you read any good books lately? What do you think of mine?").

The big trick is determining what kind of person would be most likely to be interested in your work—and since you are writing for that person, there is a large chance you will be interested in that person, too.

But what happens when your audience is an audience of one?

That's the second thing I wanted to mention: it's also entirely possible that you are writing for yourself.

And really, that is okay. I recommend this starting out, and this is how I started out myself. Unless you have a lot of people who know what your writing looks like, it can be hard to understand your audience and get feedback that will help you progress. However—because there's always a "however" for things like this—it can be difficult to get accurate feedback when you are in this position. If you are comfortable in your own pajama-covered skin and matted hair, you might never see a need to improve anything in your writing.

Setting Up Story Expectations

Since you are going to take your reader on an imaginative journey, one that they may not have experienced before, it is important to set up your story's expectations. When I was a teacher, I would metaphorically hold my students' hands as I walked them through new intellectual territories. As a writer I make that a goal as well when it comes to novel experiences. It is your job as a writer to serve as a trustworthy guide. Readers are less afraid to try your work out when you are trustworthy, and they are more forgiving when the story offers them unpleasant surprises.

That is a large part of the reason understanding your audience is so critical; if you are going to be there for your reader, it is best to make sure you are able to anticipate their needs.

This is where some marketing research will come in handy. Are you writing towards men or women, or both? What is the ideal age bracket for your audience—13-18, perhaps, or 18 and older? Kids? What are some of their interests (would they forgive some sloppy math in sci-fi, or would they be upset at "Hollywood math?") and what would motivate them to pick up a book?

There is a helpful way to determine the ideal reader we want to romance: genre.

Genre is the classification of books. Romance, mystery, fantasy, science fiction, literary fiction, poetry—these are all examples of different kinds of genre. Just by reading them, you should know which ones your story includes, and which one your story is not.

While genres evolve (or devolve) over time, some of them blend with others, and some of the founding "clichés" of each one become too cliché, the best thing you can do to find your readers is to classify your work.

We are naturally attracted to order as human beings, because it helps us understand things more quickly. We see this in a lot of high schools: We know there is a social order to the students (nerds, band geeks, jocks, cheerleaders, teacher's pets, the grunge crowds, etc.) that might only make sense to them. We see this in Hollywood too: the "good girls," the "bad boys," the "rising stars," the "has-beens." And we see this in the workplace, where there is an established pecking order in terms of company power, and we know that different people wield different social power—one of the junior partners might be the boss's best friend, so you'd have to "make nice" to him if you want the boss to like you, too, for example. Even in some families, you can see this dichotomy. If a man wants to ask his girlfriend to marry him, whose approval does he need, if anyone's? My own husband asked my mother for permission, but I know plenty of other people who had to ask the father, or sister, or brother, or even best friends.

The bottom line is that order is important to us. Everyone has their own organized madness in their methods.

So, what is your story's primary genre?

Is the focus of the plot solving a mystery (mystery, thriller)? Is it about falling in love (romance, maybe horror)? Is it about saving the world, or about fulfilling a prophecy (fantasy, adventure)? Or finding a date for prom (teen and young adult)?

Writing involves asking a lot of questions and then finding out the answers as you go along.

Once you have your audience in mind, and your selected genre ready to go, you can work on creating a story that they will like, just like how once you get to know someone you're interested in, you might organize a date they would enjoy. And, just as you want a date to get you closer to seducing your partner, you want your writing to have your reader asking—perhaps begging—for a second one.

It's time to look at more specific elements of writing that will go into your story.

CHAPTER 5
* * * *

Good Sex Starts with Good Romance
Good Stories and Sexy Stories

I never read the Carl Sagan's book *Contact,* but I was fortunate to have an astronomy teacher in high school who used it in his back-up curriculum once we were done with the regular curriculum (*Star Trek: Nemesis, An Inconvenient Truth,* and *The Core* were also among the films we watched. When I think of my education in film criticism, it always starts in his classes). In the movie, a scientist finds out that there are aliens who are sending out prime numbers over radio waves to contact other planets. There's a scene where Jodie Foster is told by some other guy who's watching the events unfold and, after they send and receive another message. When the new message is confusing, the guy tells Jodie Foster's character to look for the prime numbers in it.

"How would a higher intelligence think?" is the question he asks (I might be paraphrasing) and that's a good question to keep in mind as we discuss this part of writing.

If you are creating a new world, you are automatically a "higher intelligence" in your worldbuilding. You know about your characters, all of them, or you have the capacity to do so.

It is your job as this higher intelligence to be able to relate your story's world to your audience, and you need to relate it to them in an attractive way.

If you're going to romance your ideal reader—that is, you're going to drop a dangling, delicious idea of a story in front of their eyes and expect them to bite into it, hook, line, and sinker, then you're going to need to have a story that delivers on what it promises.

In this case, instead of the focus on your writing's theoretical foundations, or everything that goes into the story's creation, and the presentation of your work and yourself, this chapter and several of its following chapters are all about story elements itself.

If you've ever heard someone ask, "Which came first, the chicken or the egg?" and someone else should reply with, "What does it matter? I want to know why the chicken was crossing the street."

The Three "Good Story" Elements

All stories, by the nature of its reality, have three things:

1. **Setting**

    Setting is the place and time in which your plot is happening to your characters.

    This is easily the simplest story requirement to fulfill because it is already tied to your plot and characters. Even if you do not directly plan for a specific setting for your story, your characters and plot will reveal it as you write it. only tricky part about setting is making it work to your story's advantage, and usually a distinction of genre will aid you in this; for example, cozy mystery stories are usually set in smaller towns.

If the chicken is crossing the road, the setting is the road and the surrounding area (It does beg the question which road it's on, doesn't it? Someone should write a book about that.)

2. Plot

The plot is the chain of events that tells the reader what happens.

If the chicken is crossing the road, the chicken moving across the road is what happens. This is the plot of what happens—so far as we know in the beginning, anyway. What happens next is up to the writer.

3. Character

The character is the sentient being, person, alien, plant, animal, or thing that is the focus of what is happening in the story. They act on their own and in reaction to the plot.

If the chicken is crossing the road, we're talking about the chicken. That is our main character; in our case, it is more specifically a sexy chicken.

All of these elements should be present to add to the overall enjoyable experience of reading your story. Forget one (and I suppose it is technically *possible* to do so, but it's just not *good*), and you won't have much of a story to tell.

Let's dive a little further into these topics before discussion how you can use each one to take your story from "good story" to "sexy story."

Setting the Scene

Selecting your story's setting is akin to choosing a place to take your significant other out on a date. Genre does not need to influence you in choosing your setting all the time. Some settings are better than others—there is a definite advantage in having your horror story take place in the middle of nowhere; it would be easier to have the car break down and there to be limited cell phone service. It would also be expected if you have cell phone service as a concern, you would need to set the story in a time where there are such things as cell phones. But if you wanted to write a horror story set in a fast food restaurant, you could still make that work, too.

If you want to surprise your reader, make sure it's a logical one that is tied to their emotions, so it will be a good surprise (there are such things as bad surprises). If you're a man taking a vegan woman out to dinner, taking her to the all grill-meat roast buffet down around the corner might not be a good idea, even if it is your favorite restaurant. But if it's tofu night? That's a surprise that could work for your reader. I'll discuss this idea of subversion more in Chapter 9, where you use your skill to put your own spin on your story despite convention of genre or other writing elements.

The big requirement with this is that you would have to make it work. I can almost see Tim Gunn looking down at my would-be Project Runway novel assignment, telling me to "Make it work." And it really is so true. No matter which ones, your choices for your story have to make sense and be emotionally palpable, if not desirable.

This particular trait is important when it comes to both plot and character as well.

Plot AND Character, NOT Plot v. Character

Where do stories begin?

When I ask that question, I feel a little like Gene Wilder in *Willy Wonk and the Chocolate Factory*, asking, "Where is fancy bred? In the heart, or in the head?"

Perhaps Machiavelli's question would be more enlightening: "Is it better to be loved or to be feared?"

Just like you should consider yourself as "dating" your reader while you write, you should consider the action-reaction, cause and effect nature of plot and character; together, they are another set of theoretical DNA that should complement each other in writing. This is a debate that has raged for hundreds of years, noted as early as Aristotle, where in his *Poetics*, he discusses which element is more important—I do believe Plato would disagree with him whatever he said, but Aristotle believe that what happened (plot) was more important than who the character (so character) was as a person.

Even if you haven't read through Aristotle's *Poetics*, you will see there is an ongoing debate between character-driven stories and plot-driven stories. The difference between them is usually where the story starts—think about the difference between a movie like *Finding Nemo* and *Avengers*. In the former, the central character, Marlin, is an overly fearful father whose anxiety eventually pushes Nemo, his son, into a situation where Marlin loses him. His greatest fear realized, Marlin has to choose to decide what to do, and (spoiler) ends up going on a quest to find Nemo, even though it is also terrifying. In *Avengers,* the central conflict centers around a group of superheroes, who must work together to defeat a supervillain. When Loki, the villain, sets his plan for world domination in motion using the Tesseract, the Avengers rise up to stop him despite the odds against them and their own interpersonal conflicts with each other.

Since character-driven novels are about characters acting on their own circumstances, while plot-driven novels are about characters reacting to an event, you will likely have both elements in your story; one tends to dominate the other, though not necessarily.

Plot is the Logical Progression

If you want to write a good, sexy story, plot and character should play off of each other; their relationship should interdependent. In writing, this is a cause and effect relationship, or causation/causality., or act-react. For my own novels, I use act-react, but I like the language of cause and effect because it's easier to remember:

Because THIS HAPPENED, that happened.
Because THAT HAPPENED, then this happened.

When something is cause and effect, it becomes like one of those Rube Goldberg machines, where you have a series of smaller steps that start with opening a door and end up feeding your fish or catching the mouse, or, if you are a *Home Alone* fan, it's the mechanism that squeezes the nail gun trigger and shoots the nails into the bad guy's nose or dumps the bag of heavy tools onto the other bad guy's head. The audience, in watching it unfold, is fascinated and wants to see it go the whole way until the end. Because of this, plot more heavily relies on the logical definition of a story, where it is more of a "sense-making device" than an "emotional experience."

The "emotional experience" of a story comes in with character.

Sexy Characters Make Sexy Stories

When you write your story, your characters should be sexy characters.

I don't mean they should look a particular way. I mean that they should be the kind of characters that hint at something deeper upon first notice. Being "sexy," is not always about being physically attractive—not even being "attractive" means you are beautiful; it just means there is something about you that people are drawn to enough that makes them look twice, or even more.

People are drawn to beauty, but they are also drawn to secrets, mystery, justice, strength, humor, intelligence, and insight.

Characterization often needs more attention because people themselves are complicated. Shallow characterization leads to the charge of stereotyping, and that is a rabbit hole you don't want to send your critics down.

While you don't have to make your characters complicated to make them sexy to your readers, your characters should still have a believable design, and that means you should consider the universal aspects of your characters, the things that we all have in common with each other.

Four Essential Sexy Character Requirements:

1. Desires

Your character *wants* something (or doesn't want something). What is it? What the wish your character wants most?

While we will talk about conflict in the next chapter, your character should want something, and that goes along with the fact that what he wants is not something he has.

Having something to want means you are giving your character a goal for the story, and often that will lead to trouble. There's a good reason there is a mantra in Buddhism that says "Desires are our downfalls." If there is nothing your character wants, it is possible that the story can be about finding the thing she wants most.

You likely know this from your own experiences, and I know this just because you are reading this book. You want something – to be a better writer, perhaps, or you want me to stop rambling so much, or maybe you even want me to talk more about sex. Maybe you want sex in addition to wanting to be a better writer, and you thought this book was a good idea to tackle both topics at once.

2. Motivation

Your character should be motivated. You can want something, but you don't always have to be motivated to get it. For a sexy story, it's a story that remains attractive and irresistible to your reader, so your character should be motivated to find a way to get what he or she wants.

Motivation can be internal or external, or both. You want to be a better fiction writer. Maybe it's because it's your lifelong dream. Maybe it's for money. It can be both.

When you are with the special person you love, you should want to have good sex. Intrinsically, good sex offers us the strength and vulnerability of love and acceptance from the person we love most, who is special to us. Externally, your hormones will be very happy. It "is good," "feels good," and is good for us.

Your characters should likewise demonstrate these traits, both to connect to your audience on a logical and emotional level.

No one wants an unmotivated lover.

3. Values

Everyone values *something*. It can be a person, an ideal, or something else. Anything else. What you value will always be at the center of your life, whether you see it or not, and this appears in multiple places in our lives. A company will often hold key values, listing them out in their business plan or their mission statement, for example. There are the five pillars of faith in Islam that demonstrate the values it has (I use this example in determining my own values, specifically because I like the idea of being able to remember the biggest values of your life by counting off one hand). Laws are written based on priorities among a shared community, region, or nation.

With this, it is important to realize that just because your character says he values something, does not mean he actually does, or that he values it as much as he says he does. Human beings are complicated, and that means that there should be more than one value we hold and the values that we do hold are often at odds with each other.

Sex itself, in relationship terms, can be seen as a value. It is a wonderful ability to communicate love physically to your beloved, but it is possible to have sex without being intimate.

If you value something, you will sacrifice for it. What is your character willing to suffer for?

Complications can arise from further questions, such what the venue of suffering is, and how long, and how much possible reward or punishment he is risking throughout the story.

4. **Patterns**

   Whether you knew it or not, the people who know you well know you're predictable. Your character should have a default setting, where when a certain stimulus is introduced, it produces a certain reaction.

   For example, in my own life, I know how I handle stress, which is poorly, especially given my age. When I get stressed with work, I want to start a new project, because a new project is an ongoing distraction from the stress of the current project (so my demons are inbred). When I feel embarrassed, I try to deflect with humor (so that's the explanation for the demon joke and how it relates to my writing frenzy).

   You might even have established patterns when it comes to romance. Women who want to look their best can go get their legs waxed, and men who want to impress put on a tux.

Just as these are all true, your character should have a default method of both acting and reacting to what happens in their lives.

People are Complicated – and Capable of Change

While all of these things are essential to understanding your characters, and therefore being able to relate them to your audience, there is an accompanying note of importance: While people are complicated, they are also capable of change.

One of the famous quotes about stories, about character and destiny, is:

"Watch your thoughts, because they become your words; watch your words, because they become actions; watch your actions, because they become your habits, watch your habits, because they become your character; watch your character, because it becomes your destiny."

Frank Outlaw is credited for saying that.

But!

But Frank Outlaw (great name) does not mention that people *can change*. And therefore, if we accept the rest of his premise, we must be able to assume destinies can change. And that is both good and bad news for us, because it means those small things about ourselves can either help or hinder us, and sometimes we don't always know it until we're able to look back and see it.

The same is true for our characters, and we should offer that to them if we are going to be benevolent higher intelligences.

My Best Story Advice

Even if you are struggling to write a good story, the best advice I can give you is to do your best to build sexy characters, where your audience, even if they don't like them, will be unable to resist finding out more and seeing more of what they do. The other nice thing about this advice is that the characters' internal drama will often point to the type of plot progression that needs to take place to develop their character.

And that point leads us to the next topic, which is tension and conflict.

CHAPTER 6
* * * *

Tension and Conflict
I Have a Bad Feeling About This

Have you ever walked into a room where everyone was silent, and you have an awkward feeling they were just talking about you?

"Hey," you say. "Who died?"

And that's when you learn they weren't thinking of you at all.

In the last chapter, I discussed how plot and character should play off of each other, just as you would honestly adapt yourself while you were out on a date with your ideal reader. Understanding tension and conflict and how they relate to your characters can add significant appeal to your story.

What's the Difference?

There is a difference between tension and conflict. Tension is something I would compare to potential energy. It is the womb that only needs a spark to birth any number of possibilities. If you're like my future self will likely be, it's that moment when your teenager drives and your fingers dig into your armrests, wondering if traffic will be manageable.

Tension is also capable, of course, of being a good form of tension. We all love that moment of tension that leads up to a romantic kiss, or that moment where we wonder if the hero will actually triumph. If you're like me, it's that extra-long moment in *Tangled* where Rapunzel is crying over Flynn Rider's dead body and the teardrop hits his face and there's nothing long enough to make us wonder if nothing is actually going to happen.

Conflict, on the other hand, is the active wrestling of the soul. It is seen when our character is facing an obstacle, most likely preventing him from getting what he wants. There are seven different types of conflict in literature.

1. **Man vs. Man**

    A character is in a conflict with another character.

2. **Man vs. Himself**

    A character is in conflict with himself.

3. **Man vs. Nature**

    A character is in conflict with nature (storms, survival).

4. **Man vs. Supernatural**

    A character is in conflict with the supernatural (God, demons, angels, demigods).

5. **Man vs. Technology**

    A character is in conflict with a form of technology (robots).

6. **Man vs. Society**

A character is in conflict with society or social norms (social revolution, social disarray, opposing political and religious institutions).

7. **Man vs. No conflict**

   A character is faced with the possibility of conflict, but it does not arise.

If you've ever known anyone who just couldn't stay away from drama in their lives, or if you've watched any soap opera from the last twenty-plus years, you'll know why having a good understanding of tension and conflict will really help your story make your readers come back for more.

In the previous chapter, I mentioned that plot and character should play off each other, in a cause-and-effect bond. In this chapter, while conflict should also be able to pay off both plot and character, like a sexy story love triangle of sorts, the characters individual conflicts should also play off of each other.

What secrets are your characters keeping from each other? What clashing values or duties do they have that keep them apart or divided? What past experiences or present griefs influence their current decisions, actions, or thoughts? Are they growing or stagnated? What is something they are waiting for to happen? How would they describe the situation they find themselves in? How would their closest friends and acquaintances describe it differently?

How far are they willing to go for what they want? How much pain and suffering do they—or others—have

Cost, Risk, and Consideration

There is a price that you pay for everything that you do. Every choice you make, you are saying "yes" to something and "no" to something else. In your own life, when it comes to writing, you are already saying yes to the story inside of you—and that means you may have to say no to other things. To be a writer means that you will need to carve out a time to work and actually work once you've come to it.

In your characters' lives, they must also make choices. To keep your audience engaged, your characters' choices should be hard, ones that demand some kind of sacrifice and discomfort. Sometimes I think of it as a horrible game of "Would You Rather?" with my characters.

The interplay between tension and conflict, with plot and character, results in either a payoff or no payoff for your character. If it does come, there is the matter of degree in which it comes. Perhaps your story has a happily ever after, or maybe it is a Pyrrhic victory? And even if it doesn't come, there is a matter of collateral damage. Maybe it is a false happy ending. Maybe there is still hope after tragedy.

In the end, the conflict should be resolved enough that your reader is happy, because leaving things unresolved can make people feel frustrated and—

CHAPTER 7
* * * *
Don't Pick Your Nose While Making Out
It's All About Style, Baby

Imagine you are out on a date with your dream date. The moment is just right, the night is brisk and wild, but still comforting, there's music playing in your heart or running through your head, and in a moment of pure magic, you look at your date and you know.

You just know, and together as one, you both lean in for a kiss.

And then you see the huge, spit-covered cut of broccoli, tucked into their gums just between the two front teeth. It leers at you while the soundtrack to *Psycho* screeches out between your bodies.

Do you still want to kiss your date? Even if you do, are you going to be able to enjoy it when the last thing you see is a piece of food stuck between their teeth? What if you end up French kissing?

Like picking your nose while you're making out, like sneezing as you go in for a hug, and just like falling off the bed at the wrong time, it is possible to make your reader confused, repulsed, or just ruin the mood. You stop what you're doing, you stop what you're feeling, and that's it. Maybe you don't stop all the way, you're just sidetracked. Or you're confused. And then maybe you're hungry or tired or you realize you need a shower—or maybe you need to brush your teeth.

If you want your writing to be as sexy as possible, you will need to make sure that your story flows easily from one scene to the next, from one decision to another complication, to a desperate choice, to a mistake, and so on until the conclusion of the book. The books that are unable to be put down are the ones where you can read and read and there is nothing interrupting you, and everything that is keeping you absorbed in the flow of the story.

Go with the Flow

Like a powerful downstream current, if you can master flow, you can trap your readers throughout your entire story. And the best place to begin this is at the beginning.

When I taught Language Arts for high schoolers, when we would go over writing, I would mention there are some special ways to open up your introduction paragraph. Readers need a good "hook." If you look at the list I just gave (secrets, mystery, justice, etc.), you'll see that they line up with the most effective ways to open an essay:

1. Ask a question (Secrets, mystery, perhaps justice)
2. Start with a shorter story or case study illustrating your intended point (Justice, insight, humor)
3. State a fact (Intelligence, justice, secrets)
4. Offer up a well-known quote or provide a definition (Insight, intellect)

It is not that different when you start writing your story. You want to introduce your characters, set off the conflict, and get the plot rolling.

C. S. JOHNSON

Keeping the Flow Going

1. **Hook them right from the start.**

    While there is no set wrong way to start a book, exactly, there are a lot of bad ways. Your opening scene should be in line with genre requirements, along with any other standards for your intended audience (age appropriateness, vocabulary considerations, topic accessibility). What are you going to offer your audience that will get their interest in the rest of your story?

    From that point onward, you should be concerned with flow maintenance.

2. **Include what is necessary.**

    While this should go without saying, but include scenes that allow your reader to understand what is going on. The plot should logically progress, even if the characters' reactions to it are illogical.

3. **Build on as you go on.**

    As you progress beyond the beginning of your story, build on the story as you write it. If you start strong, it'll be able to hold up more as you keep going with the story.

    While plot twists can be fun, they should not be accidental.

4. **Don't include boring parts.**

   While this might seem to be the same thing as #2, it's not. "What is drama, after all, but life with the dull bits cut out," is how Alfred Hitchcock put it. Keep the boring parts where needed, but otherwise cut it. Stephen King would say "Kill your darlings" at this point.

   If something doesn't work, it's easier to drop it. If it's good enough or flexible enough, you can rework it somewhere else.

5. **Reaffirm your foundation.**

   Sometimes you want to remind the reader where your characters have been. It's good to allow them time to digest certain plot points. Like a spider's web, you'll want a silky thread that spins into one, interconnected story, and that means periodically providing hints of what happened.

   This is also helpful for providing plot twists. You can have something happen that puts an event in a new light.

6. **Include sensible jumps.**

   If you are going to jump from one character to another, or another time and place in the story, make sure it is both logical and necessary, and the reader can be transitioned in a way that is both smooth and logical. Flow requires that everything is tied together.

If you change the subject in the middle of a discussion, we can go along with it, but we have to agree with the reason for it.

7. **Use language to add beauty or humor.**

Keats is guilty of giving us the line that says, "Beauty is truth, truth beauty, —that is all / Ye know on earth, and all ye need to know," in his "Ode to a Grecian Urn," and after all that lovely use of language, it's somewhat jarring to find that he is actually wrong. Not everything is beautiful is true, and not everything that is true is beautiful. But the prettiness of his poetry makes us believe it to be so, or at least argue out the particulars. Still, people are drawn to beauty, and if you can make your work beautiful through your choice of words, do it. The same thing goes with humor, intellect, and emotion. Always seek to engage the reader with something of interest, in an interesting way.

There are related elements to flow like rhythm, mood, and tone, and most of it is related through word choice, sentence structure, and author intent. In many ways, this sort of flow is reflected in the soundtrack to movies; when the music shifts, our mood does, and sometimes it is different enough that we are pulled out of the story's flow. In writing, our words are music notes, and what we choose impacts our reader as we share that with them.

When it comes to sex, we can see how the timing of a kiss, the delicacy of a touch, and the urgency of an embrace stir our desire to add to our mutual pleasure.

While flow focuses on the importance of keeping the reader's attention, sometimes flow is intentionally disrupted for story purposes. And that is where the next topic's chapter comes in.

CHAPTER 8
* * * *

Getting Kinky with It
Adaptations & Variations

Up until now, I'm laid out the rules of the game: Good writing is like good sex, here are the things writing and sex have in common, and here's how you can use this metaphor to make your writing sexier, and here's how to make your story sexier, too.

But!

But here's the thing about rules: People break them.

It's not always a question of whether or not they should be broken, but it is a fact that people do. Sometimes they break the rules badly; sometimes they break the rules beautifully. Truly mastering the art of writing well means you know how to break the rules beautifully, provocatively, and in a way that people leave people satisfied.

Expecting One Thing, Getting Another

In Matt Groening's *Futurama*, there is an episode called "When Aliens Attack," where an alien race invades earth all to see the finale episode of a thousand-year-old TV show. In the episode, the main character offers this crucial writing advice which ends up saving the world: "Clever things make people feel stupid, and unexpected things make them feel scared … TV audiences don't want anything original. They want to see the same things they've seen a thousand times before."

When it comes to love and sex, there is an also element of familiarity that allows for that foundational trust between parties. If you want to rock the boat, you need to make sure your audience trusts you.

Your story is grounded in setting the reader's expectations. A lot of this has to do with genre; a romantic comedy will end with a happily-ever-after, or a happily-ever-after-for-now, and a mystery thriller will end with the mystery being solved and the bad guy defeated.

When you want to make a different ending to a traditional genre's expectation, you are allowing your reader to expect one thing. If you meet their expectations, you're writing safely (it can still be beautiful, clever, and satisfying.) If you exceed their expectations, you are providing what authors John C. Wright and L. Jagi Lamplighter call, "superversion," where hope is infused beyond the ending the of book and the story itself is elevated to a new level of inspiration. It takes the catharsis of the character, where the character experiences a revelation, and then pushes it to the higher levels of purgation. This is where the character sees not only the truth, but the negativity surrounding his character and the events that have happened. It is also possibly that his catharsis leads to purification, where his life will not only be better because of his actions, but he will take on new, positive learning to shape his life and the lives of others around him.

When you thwart the reader's expectations—most often in negative, unexpected way, it is called "subversion," where the character experienced a catharsis, and then chooses to negate it. Perhaps the hero is overcome, but other citizens step up and save the day; perhaps the guy gets the girl in the end, but she ends up dying. This is where the cliffhanger concerns also go; you could leave your story on a cliffhanger, with the intent to pick up the story in the next book or installation. For this one, I know from my experience not all readers are okay with this—my own mother made me promise to lay off the cliffhangers for a few series after the last one she reader.

Changing Perceptions: Plot Twists

My favorite plot twist is still from *The Office*. Andy, Dwight, and Michael are all double agents working their game of *Belles, Bourbon, and Bullets* from the episode "Murder," but it's hard to think of anyone more famous for plot twists than M. Night Shyamalan. While he works in film, the same principle applies to writing: Plot twists change the perception of the audience in a dramatic fashion, and because the perception has changed, expectations also change. There are two major points to making plot twists work for your writing.

The first requirement is subtlety. You want to have clues along the way for people to pick up on, but only realize their significance in hindsight. Ambiguity and the use of double meanings can also aid in setting your audience up for a plot twist they don't see coming.

The second thing you will need when working with a plot twist is believability. While I hate to use the 51% to 49%, your plot twist should at least be 51% believable, so you will need proper motivation for the events and the revelations. The change that's taking place still has to make sense.

A Total Turn-Off: Don't Burn Your Bridges

A necessary word of permission and caution: If you are going to adapt your story in a way that your audience might not appreciate, do it respectfully. You can still do it, but do it respectfully. If you're going to break up with someone, you would want to do it as friends, right?

If Stephen King's *Misery* has taught us nothing else, it is that you should never intentionally make your audience needlessly and excessively mad. Arthur Conan Doyle had this issue with Sherlock Holmes, where his character became so popular, he killed him off, and by audience demand, he had to go to great, logical lengths to bring him back to life.

Your audience is giving you time to read through your work. That is something to respect, not something that you should expect. When you expect something from someone that should not be given freely, that can really damage your relationship.

Additional Thoughts on Variety

There are a lot of different ways to tell a story, just like there are a lot of different ways to enjoy sex. If you find something you like to do with your writing, you can work on developing that while you still learn things.

Even now, there are plenty of things I like to change up with my writing: Tense, perspective, genre, length, and audience. While I am still learning, there are times when I will make mistakes when trying new things out. As an author, give yourself the grace to work through it, and be a writer that people can forgive, so if you need it, you have it.

You don't have to meet all your audience's expectations, but you do have to do your best.

Which brings us to the next chapter …

CHAPTER 9
* * * *
Finishing Well
Great Writing is Like Great Sex

Is there anything more disappointing than an anticlimactic finish?

When it comes to reading, I would say no, because that's the part that we tend to remember most after everything is done. We remember that the prince and the princess get married and live happily ever after, the hero's triumph or death, we remember the funeral or the wedding or the new baby on the way, and while we remember the basic elements of the plot, we like to know how it ends. That's why many people will finish a book or a movie even if they hate it.

So you need to finish well when you write. You could have the best sex in the world leading up to the end, but we all know we'd all like to get the happy ending we're searching for. And now that you have learned all about how to write a sense-making emotional experience, careful to have your plot intertwined with character, and characters who play off each other to create authentic, engaging scenes that allow your audience to sink into your story and its world, it is time to finish.

The End

Finish your story. No matter what. Bring the story to a point where all your character's troubles are solved—or solved enough—and there is some substantial degree of hope or hopelessness.

Your plot should be at a stopping point, unless you're intentionally leaving it on a cliffhanger, while your characters should be at a set place in their internal and external journeys. You want to stop at the best place for maximum reader investment and payoff; that's the time to end it. You don't want to keep dragging the audience into deep emotional turmoil without rewarding them, and you don't want to reward them needlessly. We see this this trouble with TV series a lot—sometimes they peak too early and then the rest of the series can still be good but has to work up to its former glory, or the series drags on and on and we get tired of it and then forget about it.

Your ending doesn't have to be perfect, but it does have to be good enough.

Final Touches

One of better differences between writing and sex is that while both are expressions of art and intimacy writing is able to be edited. There is no editing sex in the process unless you have a time machine and a *Men in Black* flashy-thingy.

It is much easier to rewrite and edit a story than to write one. You have the material all laid out in front of you, so you just have to move it around and tweak it to create the best story possible.

There are three topics that come up after you are finished writing your story:

1. **Rewriting**

    Rewriting, or the process of writing over your work, should allow you to check for revision needs on every level, from individual word choice to transitions between paragraph and chapters, to the overall story progression, and then, finally the conclusion.

2. **Revision**

    Revision is similar to rewriting, but there is usually more of a focus on grammar and mechanics.

    This is where having some outside help can really make a big difference in the quality of your work. A content or story editor will be able to make suggestions for genre expectations, stylistic improvements, and story inconsistencies. A line editor will focus on grammar and mechanics, and a proofreader can check to make sure your formatting is polished and professional.

    Feedback can be very helpful, and not just in this phase, which I address with the following point:

3. **Feedback**

    Feedback is the overall assessment of your writing before it is published; critical reception is what happens after publication. Feedback does not have to be professional; many friends and family members might be able to step up and offer you their thoughts on your writing when you are ready to share it.

Some writers will not reach the point where they are willing to share their work with others right away. When you are a writer, your work is often like having children, and while you appreciate feedback from teachers and babysitters and your friends, it can be difficult to accept flaws or areas that need work. Just like your relationship with your reader, you want to make sure the person giving you feedback on your story is someone you can trust—someone who has some authority on the subject, perhaps in your particular genre, or someone who knows you well and respects your efforts.

My advice for handling the question of feedback is to do with it the most care possible. It is not an easy thing to do, to ask people to read the words that come from your heart more than your mind. You should expect some feedback that is negative, and ask if there are any areas which can be improved. If you expect bad news, bad news is easier to deal with. But it is not for the skeptic to remain skeptical, any more than it is appropriate for the cynic to remain cynical; take the praise offered as sincere and treasure it. Everyone who writes is a writer, but some are more advanced in their training than others. While you may or may not have some natural talent, you are in charge of developing your weaknesses and refining your strengths. The training in question is painful but rewarding, and as you get better with intentional practice, the only regret you'll have is that it took you so long to get where you are.

While editing is a key part of writing, it should be seen as a chance to learn how to write better. It took me a long time to see editing as a way to increase my writing efficiency. One of the things people are impressed with when it comes to my body of work is that I write so much. Part of that is because I can do it faster now that I've learned from my edits. I know how to do certain things because I've done them before several times. As you work through edits, checking over all aspects of your work, you will slowly master different aspects of writing. You will find as a writer, there is always room for improvement, and if you're like me, you'll always find something new to try. If you want to be a good writer, you still have to be a writer first. And if you want to be a good writer enough, you will bear the work and its weight while you do the writing itself.

Good writing is like good sex; no one is born knowing how to do it perfectly, but there is great pleasure and reward waiting for you in the work you do. Sometimes the hardest part is to just keep going after you've had a bad day—which is where the last chapter comes in handy.

.

CHAPTER 10

*   *   *   *

Afterglow
A Job Well Done

There are a couple of things I should mention before I close out this book.

The first thing is that I wanted to thank you for reading it. If you enjoyed this book, you should let other people know about it and leave a review somewhere for it. Also, if you hated it (which I, biased as I am, sincerely hope you did not), you should leave a review somewhere, too, because that will help other people decide if they would like to give it a chance or not. Reviews are a form of feedback, and if you think there's been a problem with the book, it might inspire you or someone else to write a better book about the subject. It also helps me, perhaps, if I get reviews. If you're in the business of selling something, chances are you've heard the adage that "sex sells." Considering the massive selection of entertainment today that consists of sex, it's not a hard leap to see that it certainly carries some truth to it. But for me, as the author, I like to see the reviews just as much as I like to see that it sells.

The second thing I should mention is that while this book should give you some sexy, sexy starting points for writing a seductive story, there are plenty of other books and resources on writing, story development, and editing that I do recommend you also read if you want to be a better writer.

The following is a list of my favorite books that make me think about writing and keep me interested in what they have to say—for the most part, anyway.

Memorization is still the mother of all learning, and that means some of it has to be boring or we wouldn't appreciate the ways of Uncle Insult Comic, Pop Quizzer, Cousin Real-Life MacGyver, or our curmudgeonly odd, everyman-neighbor Stephen King.

It is the nature of good, accessible writing to be well-rounded, but being well-rounded changes as time goes on and trends morph. It's best to keep pace if you can, but it's also not a bad idea to keep the older stuff on hand. One day, it will be vintage, after all, and nostalgia comes around every twenty/thirty/forty years or so.

Provocative Resources

1. *One Big Thing*, Phil Cooke

Phil Cooke offers a deluge of wisdom and insight from his years of being in the media and working around Hollywood. I put his book first on this list because I think a lot of people want to do a lot of things, and while variety can be good, it can also hamper our progress. This book of his talks about the importance of focus on a project, working towards a specific end, and how to handle some of the surprises and stresses that come along with it. I haven't even finished writing this paragraph praising it and I'm already making the mental note to read it again.

2. *Story*, Robert McKee

If there is such a thing as a writer's Bible, in the sense that it's the book you want to check for the biggest theoretical questions and philosophical implications of story, this one is it. McKee's work is humorous, lyrical, and -- while it is long -- engaging. His insight into both film and story are spot-on for the current age, and he has a lot of wisdom to offer writers, both new and old.

3. *The Elements of Style*, E. B. White

This is quite possibly the most well-known book on this list. It's short, to the point, and helpful on a variety of topics.

There's no sex talk in it though, so be prepared.

4. *The St. Martin Handbook*, Updated Edition as Needed

While I did review some very, very, very basic grammar in Chapter 3 of this book, *please* pick up a grammar book and work through some of the initial questions of each chapter and the end of the chapter sections. It's important to have an editor check your work for errors, but you should also do your best to learn how to write things as correctly and cleanly as possible. When my editor sends back notes, I always try to make sure I correct myself with some of the patterns I see in my work. While 100% perfect grammar is not necessary for a story to become a bestseller or to be loved (and while it is unlikely you will eventually write a book with 100% perfect grammar or a book free of typos) please recognize that it is an important part of communication and that we need good grammar in order to understand each other.

There are other grammar handbooks you can buy to help you as well, but I really like St. Martin's. I have used them in my classrooms and found them to be helpful for all ages and all levels, including people for whom English is not their first language.

5. *By Cunning and Craft*, Peter Selgin

It is always good to have a go-to book when it comes to reviewing simple parts of a story or book that are not always evident. Not too many people pick up a book based on its theme, even if a theme is something that people remember from the book better than the plot itself. In this case, Slegrin's book is my go-to. He goes over ten lessons that fiction writers will benefit from. In his work, he offers several examples and goes into detail to demonstrate his points. He goes over style, theme, positioning, and revision techniques.

6. "How to Write A Story," Donald Miller

In this short ebook, Donald Miller dissects the basic steps for telling a story. He breaks down the basic element of the hero's journey (a popular plot outline) and works through each element on a personal as well as story level. One of the reasons I enjoy Miller's work is because he makes it simple and offers several familiar examples to help. This ebook is currently available for download from his website, Storybrand.com.

7. *The Hero with a Thousand Faces*, Joseph Campbell

Considering Campbell wrote the book in the mid 1900s, it should be noted that this book offers up a lot of hero development from some outdated or disproved concepts; however, there are plenty of great psychological, religious, sociological, and political angles that will help you approach your work in building up your hero's character. His focus on the universal things that bind us to humanity is ambitious, admirable, and well-executed.

Focusing on the universal allow us as writers to prepare ourselves for how we will write about it. Just like there are standards for good writing, there are standardized experiences for humanity that we share.

8. *Saving Cinderella*, Faith Moore

Much like *The Hero with a Thousand Faces,* Moore's book is included in this list to build on theoretical foundation. Her notes on the princess's journey, rather than the hero's journey, provide invaluable information on the quest for internal balance, acceptance, and self-actualization. The book also highlights specific examples of fairy tale symbolism, the failures of modern feminist criticism, and its implications for the modern era. I especially appreciated the focus on women as heroines, and no matter the genre, I highly recommend this book for anyone writing female protagonists. The fact that it's written using the Disney Princesses as examples just makes it all the more fun.

9. *How to Write a Novel Using the Snowflake Method*, Randy Ingermanson

When I first decided I wanted to be a novelist and write for money, this was one of the first books I picked up. It has a lot to offer the writer-to-be in brainstorming and fleshing out the details of your imaginary world. I've found this is a good resource for people who do not want to outline their stories (known as "plotters"), but also do not want to just start writing and let instinct take over (called "pantsers"). I am personally somewhere in between those two extremes—I say I am a "Jazzer," which reminds me of jazz music, and that means there's a whole new meaning to jazz hands that could apply to typing, so I am pretty happy with that term.

10. "An Essay on Criticism," Alexander Pope

While it is not an essay that we would know of today, Pope's poem is teaming with intellectual musings on how writing should be done and understood. He also offers advice on what should constitute mastery, and how to set your expectations for yourself as a writer. The fact that it is a poem written entirely in iambic pentameter and heroic couplets, offering the occasional line of satire, should be different enough to keep your attention.

11. *On Writing*, Stephen King

Stephen King's memoir of his thoughts on writing has been among the most recommended books for writers of all levels. I enjoyed reading some of it myself, finding it an excellent example of how the stream-of-conscious technique should be done, if nothing else. Some of it did ramble, but I can appreciate that, even if I skip over it.

12. *A Million Miles in a Thousand Years*, Donald Miller

This is, like King's *On Writing*, a memoir, but it is more about editing rather than writing—I think that's the way Donald Miller is clever; he's generic in topic but profoundly unique in his direction. Throughout this account of "editing his life," he gives us solid advice, wrapped up in his own life experiences, and then engages us with the losses, the frustrations, and the tools to keep us encouraged as we face our own hero's challenges. While I also enjoyed his *Blue Like Jazz*, this is the memoir I read for inspiration on writing. His opening line is one of the most iconic in my own reading collection: *The sad thing about life is that you don't remember half of it.*

If that doesn't hook you in, I don't know what will; seriously, what is the point of being sexy if no one remembers you?

Some of these I have read and reread several times, and others I know I need to read again. As Samuel Johnson once said, "People don't need to be taught so often as reminded."
And so, here is your final reminder: be sexy with your writing. Aim to please yourself, but also aim to give pleasure to your readers. Be provocative, enticing, worth a hundred million second looks. Be yourself, hire an editor, and write the story burning inside your soul. You never know how many people's hearts you can warm with the flame inside your own. Just like sex, writing can be scary, thrilling, a marker for achievement, and demonstrate the love you have for something in your life. But just like sex, it can lead to the creation of something that makes your life even more beautiful, terrifying, and wonderful, and what you end up creating might just change the world.

AUTHOR'S NOTE

Dear Reader,

If you've picked up this book because you've read my other books, I hope you'll be able to appreciate how much I have learned in the last several years as a fiction writer. If you are picking this book up as a new reader of mine, I hope you won't judge my other work too harshly. One of the best things about living is that you are always able to learn, and with consistent practice, you do end up learning more than you realize.

Most of you who know me know I largely started writing fiction to figure out my own internal conflicts. The sensation of writing a novel where my characters deal with similar, more metaphorical or even more literal problems than I do gives me great comfort and often great clarity. It is almost liking exorcising your own demons before you try to banish them away. Sometimes it works; your own power to name them—to call them out, and to see them, to wrestle with them in a more physical sense—is enough to send them running. Other times, you realize just how much trouble you are in, and how much power you need in order to help banish them. Thankfully, I have a great resource in Christ, even though I wrestle with the wiles of my fallen form.

The writing process has given me a great appreciation for the novels and stories that have encouraged me and allowed me to escape my life in order to find it, and so, I love nothing more than offering that to my readers in this book. The added humor is just icing on the cake, and goodness knows I love cake (especially peanut butter cake). My work is a place for your mind to play, for your heart to be encouraged, for your soul to be strengthened. I would just hope that, if the Grinch were a real person today, his heart would grow three more sizes after reading one of my books. Of course then he would likely die, because it's never good to have an enlarged heart.

While there are always surprises in life (not just in sex!), this project started as a way to encourage my readers who wanted to grow into fiction writers. My favorite novelists have not yet opened a course on how to write well (most of them are dead now, to be fair) and even though I've followed most of their advice—to which I owe George Orwell the greatest of my apologies, most likely—I wanted to provide a good starting point for mine.

While the name is suggestive and, yes, unfortunately plays to a marketing ploy, *Good Writing is Like Good Sex* is the place where I can more personally recommend that readers who want to become writers start. Yay for you! (I hope, anyway?) Even if you are not planning on being a writer, I like to think I'm funny and charming and irresistibly cynical sometimes, so it will be a good read regardless.

Since I've quoted from the books several times, I've included a sample of my work, *Kingdom of Ash and Soot*, the first book in The Order of the Crystal Daggers, my historical spy series inspired by *Cinderella*. Sometimes there is nothing more terrifying than asking to be held to the standards you have for others' work, but there is nothing more integral, either, so please check it out along with my other work and see how I do with my own standards. Here's to hoping you will see how well I've followed my own advice (or not), and here's hoping that you will begin your own writing even sooner.

Until We Meet Again,

C. S. Johnson

ABOUT THE AUTHOR

C. S. JOHNSON is the award-winning, genre-hopping author of several novels, including young adult sci-fi and fantasy adventures such as the Starlight Chronicles series, the Once Upon a Princess saga, and the Divine Space Pirates trilogy. She has written articles for The Rebelution, MTL Magazine, Hollywood in Toto, StudioJake, and more. With a gift for sarcasm and an apologetic heart, she currently lives in Atlanta with her family. Find out more and subscribe to her newsletter at http://www.csjohnson.me.

ABOUT THE EDITOR

FAITH K. MOORE is a freelance writer with publications in venues like The Wall Street Journal, The New York Daily News, and The Federalist. She also contributes regularly at PJ Media and Evie Magazine. Her self-published book, *Saving Cinderella*, is available online. Before becoming a writer, Faith taught writing and other subjects to elementary school students. Find her at https://www.faithkmoore.com.

Photo Credit: Faith K. Moore

C. S. JOHNSON

<u>*SAMPLE READING*</u>

from

KINGDOM

OF

ASH AND SOOT

BOOK ONE OF THE ORDER OF THE CRYSTAL DAGGERS

by

C. S. Johnson

Published Courtesy of Prodigy Gold Books, 2018

GOOD WRITING IS LIKE GOOD SEX

Prologue

◊

My father's hands, stained with darkened sunlight and roughened sores, were cold as I touched them for the last time.

As he lay still in his coffin, I rubbed my small hands over his, much as he had done to mine before I went to sleep each night when he was home.

"Night-night, *Táta*." I said my final goodbye softly, my lips barely moving to form the words. Not even my hair stirred, the ebony curls stilled out of solemnity.

My gaze turned to his face, as the church's robed pallbearers, silently but surely, came up beside me. I felt them surround my father's body more than I saw them, as I continued to watch his face, searching for any sign his eyes might open and wink up at me once more.

A sleeve tickled my neck. "It's time to let go, miss," one of the pallbearers whispered into my ear.

"Not yet!" I objected.

"Eleanora." The sharp voice of my stepmother, Cecilia—officially Baroness Cecilia Haberecht Chotek Svobodová of Bohemia—snapped loudly and harshly against the quiet sea of silence inside the church. "Let the men do their job."

Only after I turned to face her did her hard expression melt into one of concern.

"Please," she added more sympathetically, but I knew from the hard line of her jaw she was more concerned I would make a scene in front of the whole kingdom.

How impudent it would be of me to embarrass her with my grief.

"But Ben didn't get a final chance to say goodbye," I said, my nostrils flaring.

At the sound of his name, my brother, at twelve years of age, shifted uncomfortably on the hard pew bench. In the last few days, Ben had transformed from the smart and silly, fun-loving boy I grew up with into a cynical, unrecognizable man.

I did only what I could—I waited for his response. There was a long moment where the crowded church returned to its stifled silence, before finally, finally, Ben coughed discreetly, and spoke.

"It's fine, Nora. I've already said my farewells to *Otec*."

I grimaced at his tone; it was brusque and formal, and nothing about it suggested Ben was as heartbroken as I was.

"Come sit down, Eleonora," Cecilia insisted once more. "Father Mueller is waiting to perform the last rites."

"I'll not come down until Ben comes and says a proper goodbye to our father."

"You are embarrassing yourself in front of our family and neighbors. Even His Grace has come from Moravia to be here at your father's mass." Her voice was low and deadly.

Briefly, I glanced over at the stern-faced man who was standing next to Cecilia. The Duke of Moravia, Lord Franz Maximillian Chotek, was a cousin to both the Emperor and my stepmother. His thin, dark mustache twitched in irritation as Cecilia and I battled over the right to grieve.

"It is the honorable thing to do," I argued.

My brother sighed. In his lap, I could see his fingers clench into a fist.

"Benedict, go. If it will let us move on before Adolf's body starts to smell, then by all means, appease your sister."

I held my breath, wondering what I would do if he did leave me to send *Táta* off all by myself.

I relaxed a moment later when he reached over, almost as if he was mentally reconsidering his reluctance, and grabbed his crutch; glaring angrily at me, he hobbled less than gracefully up to the altar. I was relieved when no one muttered anything about my brother's crippled leg.

"I can't believe you're making me do this," he whispered to me. "You of all people know how I feel about *Otec*."

I frowned. "Táta was a good man. Even the king said he was a good man who protected him during the Revolution."

"Kings are quick to reward those who would die for them."

"Not all of them."

"Nora, what do you know of war or any soldier's duty?" Ben hung his head at my childishness. "It doesn't matter anyway, does it? The Germans are still in control of the Diet, and the Emperor is in his palace in Vienna, while King Ferdinand is playing with his posies all day long."

My brother was clever. In ducking his head, it looked from behind as though he was sad or even crying. The church's audience murmured a quiet approval as Ben grasped onto his crutch with one hand and put his other hand over mine, while I continued to rest it on *Táta's*.

As we stood there, I saw there was a bluish tint to my father's stiffened hands, and I wondered if death had chilled him even in the afterlife, so much that his veins had swelled. I looked back up at his face, surprised to see there were similar lines around his lips, although his beard and mustache helped to hide the unsightly marks.

"There." Ben squeezed my hand. "Are you satisfied?"

"Yes." I nearly choked out a response. "He was all we had, Ben, no matter what you say."

I slowly released my father's hands and whispered one last prayer toward the heavens for his soul as I headed back to my seat in the pew.

But when I turned around, I suddenly stopped, as a flurry of sound and movement in the back of the church caught my attention. Ben, with his uneven steps, bumped into me from behind, and I heard his mumbled curse.

Fortunately for Ben, everyone else, including Father Mueller, was too busy staring at the back of the church to chastise him.

My own mouth dropped as I saw a kingly procession entering the chapel. Men wearing fine livery made from shining threads, woven with the proud red and white colors of Bohemia, dotted the small crowd.

It was only when they parted that I saw the king.

King Ferdinand V, the former leader of the Austria-Hungarian Empire and King of Bohemia, and a string of several other titles, had arrived.

"His Majesty!" Cecilia gasped. I might have laughed at her expression at any other time, but she was right to be surprised.

The king didn't come out in public very often, and at once I could see why. My eyes took in his large forehead, his wide-set eyes, and his aged, enlarged face. His robes were grand, and his jewelry ornate, but there was nothing ostentatious enough to hide his shaking discomfort. He walked slowly, with a cane in hand and two young attendants immediately behind him for support. I, along with everyone else, including Father Mueller, stared as the elderly figure proceeded toward the front, where my father's casket was waiting.

I'd heard the rumors of the king's precarious mental state—of his simplemindedness, his mental fits. I wondered as he passed, only giving me a light glance, if he was here against his doctor's wishes.

King Ferdinand V used to be our king. In 1848, the same year Ben was born, Ferdinand was forced to abdicate his throne to his nephew, the current Emperor, Franz Joseph I.

But, as the king bowed down before the altar and made the Holy Cross over my father's corpse, I remembered King Ferdinand's informal title, Ferdinand *Dobrotivý*, or "Ferdinand the Good."

It seemed to suit him.

I blinked back tears, remembering *Táta* telling me that even kings had to bow to something greater than themselves in the end. Many of them submitted to God, in life and in death, while King Ferdinand had submitted to the power of the people. My father had remained at the king's side, protecting him from physical harm during the Revolution of 1848, when King Ferdinand's power was revoked.

Maybe that's why the king decided to come down out of his castle in the city to see him.

Father Mueller continued with the Funeral Mass, reciting the familiar lines of liturgy, along with the occasion's additions for the deceased. I barely listened to the service for my father. While grief was not preferred, it was familiar; Ben, *Táta*, and I had all been through it four years prior, when my mother was lost at sea.

As we responded to Father Mueller's reading of the twenty-third Psalm, I glanced back over at the king. My grief was great, but my curiosity was proving itself the more demanding of the two.

"I can't believe the king came," I whispered to Ben.

"He didn't come for *Máma's* funeral," he whispered, "and she was the better one between the two."

"*Táta* is with *Máma* now. They are together again at last."

"If *Otec* even made it to heaven," Ben retorted.

"Ben! That's terrible to say."

"He was a terrible man."

"To you, maybe."

"Exactly."

At the bitterness in his tone, I decided to discontinue the conversation.

But I stopped for other reasons as well—two of them, to be more precise. Priscilla, my stepsister, was earnestly tugging on her mother's skirts as she glanced over in our direction, and my stepbrother, Alexander, glared menacingly at Ben.

How can they be the same age as us, but act like such little children?

It was not hard for me to make that deduction; they had never known pain as Ben and I had. It seemed that for every burden my family had borne, our stepsiblings had only brushed theirs aside.

In addition to our mother's death, there was Ben's injury. *Táta* never forgave Ben for getting crippled two summers past, falling off the stable roof after trying to fetch one of my cats for me.

Priscilla and Alex's father, Cecilia's second husband and the one before my father, had died serving in the armed forces abroad. Even at our first meeting, Alex had been eager to boast of how his father's shield had saved the baby prince, Leopold, and his mother, Queen Victoria, and subsequently, the entire kingdom of Britain, from death and destruction. When I asked if his father was acting as a nursemaid, he nearly cried.

I think that was the moment when he began to hate me.

Quickly, so Cecilia would not see, I stuck my tongue out at Alex and glared a warning to Priscilla, before turning away from them completely.

Ben shifted in his seat uncomfortably again. I looked up to see he was giving silent warnings to our stepsiblings himself. Their derision toward us since the day we'd met had never been more inappropriate. Some part of me blamed Ben for that; he'd been angry, more angry than ever, the winter after his accident, and gaining a new family was the last thing that could have cheered him up.

"Stop fretting, Ben," I told him, placing my hands over his as I had done to *Táta's* just moments before.

"I can't. I have to watch out for you now."

I wrinkled my nose. "Cecilia's children don't scare me."

"Lucky you," he said. "There is no one to stop them from taking our inheritance now. Indeed, Cecilia has already begun raiding *Otec's* estate. How else do you think she was able to get such a fancy dress made up from the seamstress before his funeral? And how else do you think she was able to get clothes and shoes for Alex and Priscilla? I also overheard her ordering a new carriage in the English style. She fancies herself to be Queen Victoria or Empress Elisabeth, cast out to far and foreign lands."

I glanced over to see Ben was right; Cecilia's dress was indeed much finer than my own. The gown was cut in a fashionable style, though from what I remembered of *Máma's* wardrobe, I would have said it was French rather than British. The stitching was fine, and even from where we were sitting, I could easily make out the sheen of expensive silk.

"We didn't get any new clothes," I said.

"Clothes are one thing, Nora. But how will you be able to get married? You have no dowry to your name now."

"I'm not even ten years old yet."

"I knew after my accident I would never marry," Ben said. His words were stilted, as though he had to chisel them off his chest. "But you, Nora. You could have had any suitor in the kingdom, just as *Otec* said *Máma* did."

"I did inherit *Máma's* looks," I said, straightening my posture, momentarily forgetting my pain as pride took over.

"You dream of a family."

"No." I shook my head firmly. "You are my family. It is enough for me. I need no husband to be content."

"I would not let you be alone with me if you could do better."

"For all your trouble, there is no one better than you," I said. "You have always watched out for me, even before Cecilia and the demon twins came to live with us."

A small chuckle was smothered in his throat, but I heard its echo nonetheless.

"You've got *Máma's* humor too, it seems. Hopefully you'll have her strength as well," Ben said. "Because these next few years may be hard."

"*Máma* taught me to be brave, Ben. As long as you'll face them with me, we will survive." My hands tightened in his.

"We may survive, but we will not be free."

"One day we will," I vowed. "You'll see."

He could only grip my hand back in reply before Father Mueller, finished with the eulogy, harkened us once more to prayer.

" … And so, let us pray for Adolf Svoboda, a regal nobleman in the court of His Imperial and Royal Apostolic Majesty The Emperor of Austria, Apostolic King of Hungary Emperor Franz Joseph I, of the House of Hapsburg-Lorraine, his kind and generous legacy in service to His Majesty King Ferdinand V of Bohemia … "

Upon hearing his name, I glanced over at the king once more. He had his one hand resting on his walking stick, and the other nudged between his legs underneath a thick blanket.

I titled my head, watching him. Was he cold? I wondered. It was getting close to the end of summer.

When he began to twitch and moan a moment later, I felt my own body go still. "Ben, look!"

The congregation began to whisper voraciously as the king fell over in his pew, convulsing fitfully. Father Mueller faltered mid-prayer, and I saw another man, one I recognized as my father's friend and medical doctor, Dr. Sigmund Artha, hurry forward to help.

"Your Highness," Dr. Artha said. He patted down his bushy wave of gray-streaked hair, and I wondered if he had only just remembered he was in the presence of the former king of Bohemia. The faded, familiar rosary beads from the Church of St. Nicholas, the *Kostel svatého Mikuláše*, jangled against the small pack as I watched him hastily make a quick bow. "Let me assist you."

I had seen Dr. Artha in our manor enough to know that he was deathly afraid of the silliest things, from spiders and dusty books to messy rooms and babies. On several of his visits with my father, he would excuse himself to go to wash his hands, and he would rub down his hair in both a nervous and necessary habit. I found it amusing and endearing that Dr. Artha had no fear of approaching King Ferdinand.

"We're here, too, sir." One of the young attendants, the shorter one, behind the king, stepped forward.

The first attendant, the one with black hair, began to issue orders to the king's men. Meanwhile, the other one who had spoken with Dr. Artha, a slightly shorter boy with copper hair, stepped up beside the king and began to tend to him, whispering into his ear. I saw he had a small decanter in his hand.

"Stay calm, Nora," Ben whispered beside me, as the king let out a loud moan.

"Father." The second assistant suddenly yelped as the king fell to the side.

I frowned. King Ferdinand had no children.

"Father Mueller," the black-haired boy called, his voice more confident and urgent, and I quickly realized my misunderstanding. He was calling for the priest. "Please, continue on. His Imperial Highness would benefit from your godly prayers."

The other boy nodded, and the reverend complied. I saw Father Mueller's face was white with slight panic as he stepped back up to the pulpit.

As the normal prayer resumed, this time louder and clearly more strained, I kept glancing over at the king.

"Oh, merciful infant Jesus! I know of your miraculous deeds for the sick. How many diseases you cured during Your blessed life on earth ... "

I made the sign of the cross over me, still watching as the king slowly reverted to his previous state; there was less jolting and gasping, and his eyes, even though they were still blinking fast, seemed more alert. He watched the copper-haired attendant with a tepid smile on his face.

That was when the attendant boy caught my eye. He was dabbing the king's head with a handkerchief, carefully and calmly, almost lovingly, before the king whispered something. Then the boy turned to see me staring at him.

Remembering my father's affection for the disposed king, I gave the boy a kind smile.

He went still, staring at me. I stared back.

Just as I noticed he seemed to be close to Ben's age, the other attendant stepped in front of him.

"Guard," I heard him call. "Prepare His Highness' coach for departure. We will be leaving shortly. The king needs his rest."

A guard saluted him and headed down the back of the small church.

From where I was, the dark-haired boy narrowed his gray eyes in my direction. From his expression, I could tell he expected me to turn away or bow my head in feigned prayer.

Rather than submit to his wishes, I stared back at him, arching my brow at him, letting him know, in my own small way, he had no moral authority to shame me. As a citizen, I had just as much concern for our king's health, even if he was no longer our ruler.

Our imagined conversation did not seem to be going as smoothly as he might have hoped. The boy at least seemed unnerved by my response, blushing quickly and then turning back to say something to Dr. Artha, who seemed to be asking him a question.

"Nora," Ben whispered. "Stop causing trouble."

"I didn't do anything," I said.

"Just be quiet and focus on the ceremony, would you, *ségra*? Maybe it was nice of the king to come, but it seriously doesn't matter."

I was really tempted to pinch him for his flippancy. But hearing his pet name for me softened my resolve. It had been awhile since he'd called me *ségra*, and I was glad to hear it again. I took his hand in mine, holding it as I returned my focus to Father Mueller.

" ... Extend your most holy hands, and by your power take away all pain and infirmity, so that our recovery may be due, not to natural remedies, but to you alone ... "

I sighed. Father Mueller's prayers were appropriate, I supposed, but they were as dead to my ears as the words were to my heart. I knew they were for my father's heavenly ascent, but I felt Ben and I needed prayers more than our father did.

I tightened my grip on Ben's hand and prayed.

Please, Holy Father, help Ben and me. Help us to find a way to be happy once more. Please keep us together and keep us safe.

As my father's casket was finally removed from the church, as Cecilia wept loudly, kneeling before the benign king of Bohemia, as I sat helplessly next to my brother, I beseeched God again with a barrage of earnest prayers.

It would be many years before I believed God had heard me—and even more before I realized that he had bigger plans than I could have ever imagined, and he had already set them in motion.

C. S. JOHNSON

Thank you for reading! Please leave a review for this book and check out www.csjohnson.me for other my other books and updates!

www.ingramcontent.com/pod-product-compliance
Lightning Source LLC
Chambersburg PA
CBHW020141130526
44591CB00030B/171